TODAY I CHOOSE TO BE...

To: Jen

" WE MUST BECOME WHAT WE
WISH TO TEACH." -NATHANIEL BRANDEN

MARCUS LUCY

ISBN: 0-9983143-1-5
ISBN-13: 978-0-9983143-1-0

TABLE OF CONTENTS

DEDICATION

I dedicate this book to my parents, Jonah and Bessie Lucy. To the two people that sacrificed everything in service of teaching and molding me with an undeniable belief that I could be anything. To you, I credit every fiber of my existence.

Mother, because of you, my faith is indefatigable, impregnable, and industrious. When times were most treacherous, thank you for always displaying love, unbound joy, and diligence wrapped in spiritual fervor.

Father, God bless and rest your soul, you exemplified power, grace, calm, benevolence, and genius. You're synonymous with spiritual soldier. You literally worked yourself to death just to spark the world with so much light.

For as far back as I can remember, I've never heard a negatively charged mumbling word out of either of you. The completion of this book represents my celebration of you...thank you for being all that I needed and more. I love, appreciate, and humbly bow to you both.

INTRODUCTION

Initially I started documenting daily messages in service of consciously healing myself. At the time I was suffering from breakdown after breakdown as a result of various tribulations and unhealthy habits obtained from years of being a victim of my emotions. Through this daily practice, I started accepting my emotional state and sharing my experiences with people close to me. I slowly began to acquire a newly found strength and was able to empower myself through the pain, instead of being victimized by feelings. This training transformed my perspective on life enhancing my experiences and personal growth, and unveiling my gift and purpose in life.

It became apparent others utilized my story as guidance to begin their own spiritual restorative process, and I was impacting the world in a positive way. Constantly people talk about what they "wish" they could do or what they "want" to do, but there's always a gap with the actual actions that take place. With this book, I hope to help people breakthrough the obstacles that impede their progress; while building the bridge between their dream and reality. Through daily practice of establishing your choice for the day, you become responsible for self, and the gaps and opportunities for improvement become clear. Accepting to "Choose" a behavior no longer makes you a victim of circumstance or prey to your story, but a conqueror of tribulation and a powerful force. You are equipped with tools to establish integrity ensuring your thoughts, words, and actions are in sync.

We are ever changing and forever evolving individuals. Just as the Seasons continue to cycle and nature learns to adapt advancing the ecosystem, we must do the same as people. Instead of running from change, we should want to embrace and be responsible for our theories, emotions, and actions. With every day you CHOOSE a different skill to focus on while creating a deeper awareness of self.

SEASON 1

ACCEPTANCE & FORGIVNESS

ACCEPTANCE

January 1

Today I choose to be A COPYCAT CREATION. The ego is enthralled by its governing body, the extremely delicate light that seems too perfect for this world. It acts as an imitator and closely mimics the mind's every thought, translating them into physical movement. The body is merely a device used to carry out particular functions dictated by the mind. So I'll live in the world of ACCEPTANCE, using what I have in order to BE what I need. My power lies in my ability to imitate my highest self, which enables me to be aware through observation and inquiry of the embodiment of my existence simply as a vehicle for change.

January 2

Today I choose to be SUBJECTED TO CHANGE. All things are prone to be affected by the transformation of our collective manifested thoughts. Whether I accept the truth of my reality or not, it's inevitable that everything is forever continuously evolving; nothing remains the same. It is without exception that each and every moment creates an opportunity to experience something new. Instead of fighting what is certain to happen, I will channel my energy through optimistic preparation, always remaining ready to entertain fresh ideas. Doing so will drastically reduce my odds of becoming disappointed by the strong beliefs of inaccurate predictions that are set in stone under false pretenses. My power lies in my ability to remember my mind is much more effective like a parachute; when open, it allows wisdom and consciousness to serve as the resistance necessary for coercing safe flights and soft landings.

January 3

Today I choose to CLEAN HOUSE. Before I start judging the devil and expressing just how much of a liar he's alleged to be, let me first take a look at and inside of myself, evaluating just how dishonest I've been to myself and others! I AM consciously aware that we all fall short in one way or another and we can only see in others what we see in ourselves. If I have a problem with something outside of me, I will seek to understand and be the change I desire to see. I've learned that regardless of one's earthly position, male/female, black/white, gay/straight, Jew/Gentile, etc., we will all meet the same death, so why not live and love? My power lies in my ability to BE ALIVE in my own life, accepting and loving all things just as they are.

January 4

Today I choose to be A REALITY CHECK. When assessing the extent of the ramifications of my past, I like to be proactive in my approach because I AM a reflection of those previous scenarios. A daily assessment to determine if my circumstances and expectations conform to the facts of my existence is essential for adequate growth. Doing the same thing over and over but expecting different results defines insanity. I have absolutely no desire to smash my hopes and dreams by momentarily ignoring what I AM. Carefully managing my mindset in this moment is paramount in my future success or failure. My power lies in my ability to know who, what, and where I AM.

January 5

Today I choose to MANAGE EMOTIONS. Controlling my subjectively natural instinctive way of being doesn't mean ignoring those mental and/or physical sensations. Through trial and error, I've become more knowledgeable of identifying my internal disturbances and acting on them when appropriate. We must become familiar with our instinctive reactions. Many times, I've been at the mercy of my remorseful mental state, unaware of the why behind my what. Instead of always reacting to life as it unfolds, I started asking myself how I felt and addressing each cognitive and motor response consciously. Doing so allotted me the opportunity to logically and truthfully work through situations as opposed to letting them build up and intensify. My power lies in my ability to know that in order for me to take control of my own life, I need to first take a look at myself, putting pride aside, and make decisions that not only positively serve me now, but also later.

January 6

Today I choose to be CORE BELIEFS. If my life is being guided by something other than what I say I believe in, naturally I lack faith, trust and confidence in my capability to be all that I AM. I clearly haven't accepted the infinitely abundant spiritual potency bestowed upon my physical existence. Instead of acting with authority, I am allowing myself to be a fearful victim. Eventually my tolerance for allowing myself to be drawn away from my life's inherent reason for BEING would reach its threshold and the hostile conflict carried by my ego would subside. My power lies in my ability to be cognizant of the fact that I've always proven myself right, whether my focus was courageously or apprehensively supported.

January 7

Today I choose to be A SHOT IN THE DARK. When my context reflect "What is the point of life? I didn't have a say in choosing my family, no one will ever truly understand me, and my death is imminent", it appears as if there is little hope of success just making it through each day without encountering any hurt, harm, or danger. I AM still roaming this earth and I AM making a conscious effort to BE more than I've been. Being fearful has done little to nothing for the achievement of my goals. I have absolutely nothing to lose but everything to gain by giving maximum effort toward everything I think, say, and do! My power lies in my ability to know that at least once a week, yesterday is a canceled check, tomorrow is a promissory note, and today is cash in hand!

January 8

Today I choose to be A HARD PILL TO SWALLOW. At times, I've felt that my life was some kind of cruel and unusual punishment. How did I get trapped inside this body? Why do I have to live this way? Will I ever achieve my deepest desires? Even though there are more than seven billion humans on earth, why do I often feel so alone? What is the point of it all? Miraculously, once I stopped incessantly asking so many questions, I granted myself time to answer them. I then became cognizant that regardless of how much pain I've endured, how much trouble I've created, and how many times I've let myself and others down, I AM still ALIVE! I have developed a single-minded loyalty to my Highest Self and without any concerns of my past, present, or future circumstances, I AM devoted to the purpose of my being! My power lies in my ability to unlock the mysteries of my TRUE power by channeling my inner QI and accepting all things just as they are.

January 9

Today I choose to be COMPLIANT WITH MY CURRENT CONCRETENESS. At all costs, if I have any desire to grow beyond my contemporary state of being, I must take action and consent to accept where I AM. What is being offered to me is solely based on decisions I made in my past. I need to be reminded that although I won't always understand why, that doesn't hinder my competence to agree with and/or affect my present circumstances. My power lies in my ability to know that what is, is just that, but my reactions to what is, is my responsibility.

January 10

Today I choose to be A FORMATIVE ASSESSMENT. Self-reflection is imperative for improvement. In order to fully immerse myself into the evolutionary process, I need to center my intentions around gradual development, if I have any desire to maximize my life's potential. Admittedly, we've arrived at a place in this world without any substantial sensibleness, that people feel a need to attempt to rush success and expect instant gratification. This way of living reminds me that all things manifested were done so through a series of thoughts, words, and actions. My power lies in my ability to start with the man in the mirror.

January 11

Today I choose to be INSTANT GRATIFICATION. I've been under the impression that I should have what I want right now. I've acted as if I was a caveman facing life or death situations, seeking food, shelter, and defending my territory. But if I take a look back in history, I would notice that it took years, decades, and centuries for greatness to occur. Instead of figuring out ways to diminish my wisdom, wealth, and success by rushing the process, I will be sure to keep my SELF-IMAGE in line with what it took for me to BE what it is that I AM. I will no longer sabotage my own success by contaminating my plan with short-term thinking. My power lies in my ability to not mortgage my future for immediate satisfaction because doing so will always lower my overall quality of life in the process.

January 12

Today I choose to be REMEMBERANCE. I joyfully recall all those who have helped me along my path. I relish in blessings previously bestowed on me and those I have bestowed on others. I insightfully make connections between past events and their contribution to my current degree of enlightenment. My power lies in my ability to honor each chapter of my story.

January 13

Today I choose to be BLESSED. If I took the time to account for all the divine sanctions that have come my way, I would soon find that they are decidedly innumerable. I have an abundance of things to be thankful for. My life is bountiful. I continue to receive infinite gifts from the Universe. My power lies in my ability to recognize my good fortune.

January 14

Today I choose to be DELIBERATE. I leisurely ponder the details of whatever venture of opportunity life is currently presenting me. I consider from all angles what the possibilities are, recognizing the potential for more than just the obvious or immediately presumed outcomes. I suspend judgment for the time being to locate and accept contentment from the information available, knowing that an answer will come to me in a moment of least effort. My power lies in my ability to think now and decide later.

January 15

Today I choose to be NOW OR NEVER. There have been mornings I've emerged from my state of sleep, and all I could think is why has happiness eluded me for so long? Do I really desire for it to be a part of my everyday life? What is it going to take for me to obtain what has had a tendency to evade my grasp so consistently? I guess what they say is true, I can only be where I AM. I must enduringly accept my current reality and incessantly ask myself "What is my best case scenario right now?" I vow to live in the moment and I've concluded that it's my time to shine! My power lies in my ability to speak now or forever hold my peace.

January 16

Today I choose to be A COHABITANT. I gracefully coexist with others, sharing in the rich resources of The Universe. I am part of the world's community, a fiber in the greater fabric of Divine Expression. My life is interwoven into the paths and fates of infinite collective souls and co-creators. My power lies in my ability to embrace my role in the macrocosmic agenda.

January 17

Today I choose to be SELF-AWARE. I take time to contemplate myself, considering my positive and negative attributes and beliefs. I assess my expectations of others. I evaluate my reasons for desiring specific behaviors from them in an effort to illuminate the need I'm attempting to fill with their responses to me. I reflect upon the circumstances in my life and my role in creating them. By exploring primitive or disenchanting aspects of myself, I discover paths to growth and actualization. My power lies in my ability to locate my faults and nurture them into pillars of applicable wisdom.

January 18

Today I choose to be MULTIDIMENSIONAL. I am a complex being with infinite talents and applications. My gifts, interests, and attributes are abundant and ever increasing. I perpetually evolve on the physical, mental, and spiritual planes. My intellectual and emotional repertoires expand every day. My power lies in my ability to realize that I am only limited to the degree that I restrict myself.

January 19

Today I choose to be IN AGREEMENT. I seek to create coalescence and diffuse discord. I enthusiastically embrace the Divine Plan for my life as it unfolds moment by moment. I recognize that it is more advantageous to consent with the present and move forward than to dissent and dwell. My power lies in my ability to harmonize with circumstances and people.

January 20

Today I choose to be A CELEBRATION. I jubilantly honor that which is good in my life. I allocate time and effort to explicitly take joy in the many blessings I have received. In this moment, I AM in full acceptance and appreciation of my fortune. My power lies in my ability to take pride in my prosperity.

January 21

Today I choose to be GIFTED. I am adorned with a unique set of skills that I execute in a truly extraordinary way. Others are in need of my talents and are grateful for the service I provide. I have a special purpose in this world and my contribution is significant. My power lies in my ability to identify what it is I do best.

January 22

Today I choose to be IN THE MOMENT. I appreciate that which I have today instead of ruminating on that which I lack. Although the future is in my thoughts, I embrace the present and fully allow myself to enjoy the plethora of goodness that is available to me right now! I seek to experience all the beauty that is found in every step of my journey. My power lies in my ability to make use of my immediate resources.

January 23

Today I choose to be SEEING THE COMMON THREAD. I realize that singular notions and concepts can be expressed in diverse ways. I appreciate that people often seek to promote similar ideas through their own unique process. I acknowledge that different understandings may yield the same result. My power lies in my ability to derive messages without getting wrapped up in their packaging.

January 24

Today I choose to be UNDER CONSTRUCTION. I AM in the process of manifesting my full potential. I am proud of where I am and excited about what's to come. With each day, I become wiser, stronger, and more abundant. My power lies in my ability to allow for improvements.

January 25

Today I choose to be LISTENING. There is much to be learned if I quiet myself and allow others to speak. One of the greatest gifts I can give someone is the opportunity to be heard. Through my silence, I create a void that can be filled with the revelations of another's heart. My power lies in my ability to graciously receive others' words.

January 26

Today I choose to be HEAVEN. I AM the highest state of reality, a psychological paradise. I AM love, peace, and bliss incarnate. All is in complete harmony in my realm. My power lies in my ability to be transcendent.

January 27

Today I choose to be A DETECTIVE. Everything in my external experience provides clues for what I believe about myself and the world around me. The people in my life, my state of health, and my financial situation are reflections of my thoughts. By assessing the evidence, I AM able to better understand the mystery that is MYSELF. My power lies in my ability to bring into consciousness that which is subconscious.

January 28

Today I choose to be THE ONE. I AM the perfect person to execute the task at hand. I have the precise skills, knowledge, and approach to cause the necessary effect. I AM the right person in the right place at the right time. My power lies in my ability to recognize my calling.

January 29

Today I choose to be UNASSUMING. I recognize that what I don't know is far greater than what I do know. There is no limit to the knowledge I can attain, as long as I perceive myself as a student. I AM open to new information, new ideas, and new beliefs. My power lies in my ability to prioritize enlightenment over ego.

January 30

Today I choose to be HONORING MY UNIQUENESS. I acknowledge that each being in existence is infinitely distinct and complex. Although others may inspire me, I refuse to compete or make comparisons to them. I relish in my individuality. I refuse to waste energy coveting the paths of others; I focus only on the beauty of my journey. My power lies in my ability to embrace the Divine Plan for my life.

January 31

Today I choose to be POETRY IN MOTION. I go with the flow instead of fighting the current. I gracefully float along the stream of my desires. I AM relaxed and confident as I follow the path of least resistance. My power lies in my ability to be nonresistant.

February 1

Today I choose to be DISREGARDING THE STATUS QUO. I recognize that although it is tempting to be part of the crowd, I don't belong there. Following in others' footsteps is not the most efficient use of time. My goals, desires, and aspirations can only be awakened through my stream of consciousness. What works for some will not work for all. My power lies in my ability to appreciate my individuality.

February 2

Today I choose to be PATIENT. I AM at peace as I await my future, confident that my dreams are in the process of coming true. I have no need to rush, as I understand that this very moment is part of my total story. I fully accept that my desires will materialize at the right time. My power lies in my ability to trust the Universe.

February 3

Today I choose to be ADAPTABLE. I AM able to cope with new situations by finding creative solutions to any problems I encounter. I remain confident regardless of the circumstances I AM dealt. I AM open to change and I refuse to cling to conditions. My power lies in my ability to decide how I perceive events.

February 4

Today I choose to be EXERCISING SELF-CONTROL. I will not allow myself to react to situations. I will take my time choosing my response. I realize that my emotional state is determined by how I decide to perceive my experiences. I AM intentional and consciously monitor my thoughts and motivations. My power lies in my ability to determine who I AM and act accordingly.

February 5

Today I choose to TAKE RESPONSIBILITY. I refuse to blame others for my choices. I refuse to allow my past to dictate who I AM today. I AM the only person who is able to make changes in my life and accountable for my actions I AM. My power lies in my ability to be liable for me.

February 6

Today I choose to ACCEPT THE NOW. I realize that I AM where I AM as a result of my choices to this point. I AM not hung-up on what could have been or what currently isn't. I know that all I have control of is myself in this moment, but also recognize that this instant is the most powerful place to be. My power lies in my ability to perceive my circumstances in a way that allows me to be at peace.

February 7

Today I choose to SEIZE THE DAY. In this moment, I choose my path. I AM decided in my intention and enthusiastic in my actions. I move certainly through the hours of the immediate future, accomplishing my agenda effortlessly and effectively. My power lies in my ability to channel my emotive energy into my efforts.

February 8

Today I choose to be EASY-GOING. Whatever situations I encounter today will be positive. Success will be effortless. Abundance will just happen to manifest into my experience. I will maintain peace of mind and anything stressful or negative will become foreign to me. My power lies in my ability to look forward to the gifts of today, knowing that my only task is to receive.

February 9

Today I choose to be STEADFAST. Regardless of what life path I decide to take, obstacles and personal issues will be sure to follow. However, I couldn't be any more unconcerned with what I don't have and who I'm not. I AM aware that my life has purpose but KNOWING is only half the battle. So I will display persistence in all courses of my actions. My every step will be backed by a continuance of grace. I have been blessed with an unyielding stick-to-it mentality. I AM perfectly aligned with the intention my Creator originally had in mind. My power lies in my ability to know that although my glass may appear to be half empty to you, it's running over to me.

February 10

Today I choose to be COOPERATIVE. Seeking and living my life based on my Highest Self has become my sole focus. I refuse to be anything other than agreeable. I can only see in others what I see in myself. We have more compatible characteristics than drastic differences. My power lies in my ability to remain free from assumptions, judgments, and attachments.

February 11

Today I choose to be EASY STREET. Some would describe this place as a state of financial comfort and security. However, it's so much deeper than material goods and currency alone. I've learned that my body will not do anything my mind does not instruct it to do. Instead of spending the bulk of my time on external affairs, the center of my attraction is targeted on the simple pleasures of life which include placing myself first. I have chosen to be compulsively dependent on high spirits, exuberance, prosperity, and maintaining my peace of mind. My power lies in my ability to know that life is a journey and not a destination.

February 12

Today I choose to be GRAVITY. I've decided to live my life through the eyes of ambition, purpose, and calculated design for others and myself. I AM the force that keeps me grounded on earth. The more internal substance I possess, the greater my force of attraction will become. I will continue to develop the ability to draw others closer to the core of our TRUE existence. My power lies in my ability to recognize I AM and will always be the invisible phenomenon that is attractive between all existing things.

February 13

Today I choose to be PERCEPTION. I have been blessed with the ability to see, hear, and be aware of my surroundings, but this does not give me the right to judge myself or others. Although my intellectual insight has been deemed as truth, I realize that my scope is limited to my emotionally based inner experience rather than fact, more often than not. I will allow the abstract nature of the world around me to be as it is, allowing discernment to guide my beliefs, discussions, and daily activities. My power lies in my ability to take an unbiased approach toward life and all it brings my way.

February 14

Today I choose to be CONFIRMATION. No longer will I believe, suspect, or fear that I am not what I AM. My TRUTH has been established and I have reached a state of assurance that forecasts the cold hard facts of life. Every breathing moment affirms that the HIGHER POWER in me is alive and well. Love and truth don't hurt. Statements like that derive from darkness. Corroborating my life with that of the universal verifiable divine intelligence feels more empowering. My power lies in my ability to realize that I've always been exactly what I've needed to be precisely when I required it most!

February 15

Today I choose to be THE SUM OF MY EXISTENCE. When I decide to treat myself better, others choose to follow. I need to set the bar for what I desire my life to become. Breaking commitments I previously made with the Universe does not positively serve me in the short term. Lying to myself and others (regardless of how small/large) isn't optional and tightening my inner circle of friends are two actions essential for maximum output in the absence of stress. The removal of judgment, spitefulness, and egocentric behavior from my day-to-day activities can keep the weight off of your shoulders. This process allots significant surpluses of success in all stages of my life! My power lies in my ability to apply the fact that all causes are followed by effects.

February 16

Today I choose to be SERENDIPITOUS. I have been known to possess a certain stroke of luck. From the outside looking in, people typically perceive my discoveries to be unexpected and fortunate. Personally, I realize that nothing I've experienced was by accident; however, I do live a highly favorable life. I have and will continue to heavily benefit from being disposed to take the most positive view of events, regardless of the circumstances, expecting the most reassuring outcome. When I combine purposefully intended thoughts, words, and actions with my abnormally optimistic approach to all aspects of life, the aftermath, more often than not, will result in my favor. My power lies in my ability to accept the fact that all things are possible; there is nothing new under the sun, and I incessantly deserve nothing short of unparalleled greatness.

February 17

Today I choose to be THE MIRROR THAT HAS TWO FACES. Although I have the ability to perceive things in their ACTUAL state of existence, I've based my reality on what I THOUGHT it should be. Doing so has led me to a world filled with hate, pain, and heartbreak. Now that I've familiarized myself with egotistical demise, I will no longer accept the short end of the stick, and optimism is my new mode of operation. My power lies in my ability to "accept the things I cannot change, courage to change the things I can, and the wisdom to know the difference."

February 18

Today I choose to be RESURRECTED. This is the day that the shame of my past will be buried, immediately freeing me from judgment, victimization, and fear. I AM ALIVE and in control of my own life. My mind is healthy and my decision-making will reflect perfect reason. No longer will I choose jealousy, envy, selfishness, or greed as my motivating source of fulfillment. My power lies in my ability to realize that everything in existence on the face of this earth belongs to the Universe and can be taken away just as fast as I was privileged to receive it.

February 19

Today I choose to be A NEW DREAM. What if I could forget everything I've ever learned and started living a life comprised from my own creation? What if I could see the LOVE in myself like I see in others? What if I no longer had to justify and/or defend who I was, am, and what I desire to be? Call me crazy but I believe that my perception of reality is mine and I have the power to change it at any time. Whether it is perceived as the Promised Land, Nirvana, or Heaven, it is my new way of LIFE. My power lies in my ability to see that although I can look at my life and find many excuses to suffer, I will not locate a good reason to suffer.

February 20

Today I choose to be HEALING. I will focus my love and energy on myself and also meditate on others who are in need of some reconciliation. I recognize that the only person that preyed upon my demise of good fortune is me, and blaming someone or something does not absolve me from personal responsibility. My power lies in my ability to end the employment of effects, which will in turn capture my concentrated conceptions allowing me the capacity to CURE the CAUSE.

February 21

Today I choose to be PROACTIVE. I will create and control the situations that occur in my world by causing something to happen rather than responding to it after it has happened. No need I have to react to others or events. I will evoke my path to righteousness by allowing my sixth sense to carefully guide and calculate the steps I take. My newly found aggressive, passionate, and take-life-by-the-horns attitude will lead me directly to the previously envisioned end results that inspired this journey initially. My power lies in my ability to separate 'what is' and not 'what I think it should be.'

February 22

Today I choose to be SELF-WORTH. I now know that others will only treat me how I feel I deserve to be treated. I will no longer second guess my thoughts and actions because I realize that I possess the confidence and necessary skills needed to become whatever it is I desire to be. My perspective of myself is no longer cloudy or judgmental. My power lies in my ability to realistically respect and gradually but firmly establish an amicable impression of who it is I really am!

ACCEPTANCE

REFLECTION:
1) Define acceptance.
2) What have you not accepted others and/or self for?
3) What do you receive by not accepting self/others?
4) What behavioral patterns do you notice when you do/don't accept circumstances?
5) What emotions are you experiencing? If negative, what changes are needed to evolve?
6) What fears exist because of your lack of acceptance of self/others?
7) If you applied empathy and compassion to this moment, what would it create for self/others?

CHOOSE TO ACT:
1) Practice releasing the desire to feel superior, gain revenge, or be the victim. Get responsible for your thoughts, words, and actions independent of external factors.
2) Practice extracting the positive lessons learned from the experience(s) that previously led to heartache.
3) Practice seeking understanding by visually experiencing the other person's situation from their perspective. Empathy breeds connection and growth.

<u>FORGIVENESS</u>

February 23

Today I choose to be FORGIVENESS. I realize that nothing positive will come from hanging on to anger, resentment, or pain. I free myself by detaching from the wrongs that others have inflicted on me. I am no longer imprisoned by past events. My power lies in my ability to know that despite the fact that all of us are perfect as is, none of us are without flaw!

February 24

Today I choose to be EXONERATED. Throughout my life, I've been tried time after time. I've judged myself beyond belief. Not only did I commit the unfulfilling acts, I also took the liberty of sentencing myself by confining my mind, blaming myself for a fault or wrongdoing. I found myself poisoning my consciousness by consuming my thoughts with negatively charged notions convincing myself that even though I didn't know what I didn't know, somehow, I was supposed to do better. Well, the mere fact that I AM breathing, alive and well, is a testament to my TRUE strength. I am as free as I perceive myself to be. My power lies in my ability to obtain a willingness to hold myself accountable for my own success because I've learned that when I value freedom above other things, naturally, I'll make more logical decisions aligned with my integrity.

February 25

Today I choose to be EASY COME, EASY GO. I've gotten so accustomed to worrying and stressing over all that 'COULD' go wrong, I haven't taken much time to reflect on what IS already going right. For one reason or another, I didn't make the 'WHATS IF's' work in my favor. Like Siamese twins, self-defeating negative self-talk and I had somehow become intertwined and linked together. At some point, enough is just enough. I'll opt out of always persecuting myself for any and every little thing. As a substitute, I'll decide to beseech myself for help hawkishly focusing on the bigger picture. I'll embrace risks knowing that every breath I breathe coerces me to be the perfect target for life and death at the same time. Whether I am aware of my all-encompassing greatness or not, I am and have been stronger than all I've been through in my past. Otherwise, I would cease to exist! My power lies in my ability to open my eyes in the midst of darkness emulating a moon that's full realizing that STILL, I SHINE.

February 26

Today I choose to LET BYGONES BE BYGONES. If I AM supposed to treat my neighbor(s) like I do myself, I must first decide and define how I desire to be treated. Doing so will form my thoughts, which will shape my words, and as a result, provide the imperative infrastructure needed to allow people to BE just as they are, even when they behave in ways that I don't. When I have achieved this emancipated state of existence, I will naturally forgive all of the people I've wrongly accused of hurting me in my past. In retrospect, they were simply mimicking the way I cared for myself, or lack thereof. For that reason, I AM no longer a victim of circumstance. My power lies in my ability to ignore and disregard all past offenses when dealing with myself and other individuals.

February 27

Today I choose to be the FRUITS OF MY LABOR. At times during my disillusioned and unconscious past, I've displayed disappointment, disdain, and dismay I felt like my actions were not yielding the results I initially expected. I further punished myself by expressing unfavorable and adverse judgments toward my self-worth, criticized my intelligence, and condemned my character indicating a strong disapproval for the consequences of my previous deeds. What I failed to realize was that every time I added uninformative feelings to my then present circumstances, I simply prolonged the manifestation of my mental imagery. For lack of a better term, I was my own cancer. I now know that ALL things take time to materialize. When I stop allowing the antagonistically fearful thoughts of what isn't currently present in my life to negatively influence my mind's focus and start being appreciative for what it is I do possess, my hard and diligent work will then pay off. My power lies in my ability to know that my season of increase is NOW.

February 28

Today I choose to be A U-TURN. My life had been up and down to say the least. I have been beaten, battered, and bruised by the barbarity and bloodthirstiness of my ego. I got to the point where I just couldn't get any lower; I was at my wit's end. Let me tell it, I struggled mightily and hadn't lived up to my true potential. Then logic set in and it dawned on me, if those previous sequence of events were so arduous, why am I still alive? Regardless of how bad I thought it was, somehow I still EXIST. So I altered my thoughts and my world took a complete reversal of direction of travel. These days, my beliefs, my uttered sounds, and my actions are heavily supported by the ultimate synthetic state of consciousness. My power lies in my ability to know that as long as I'm breathing, I still have an opportunity to BE.

February 29

Today I choose to be ABSOLVED. I free myself of all shame and guilt from lower acts I have committed against others and myself. I realize that the poor or unenlightened choices I have made in the past, and the lessons they delivered, are part of my journey to greater freedom and understanding. I release any negative energy associated with my earlier stages of self-development and make the decision to focus on how far I have come. My power lies in my ability to forgive myself.

March 1

Today I choose to be FED UP. I have done this song and dance long enough and honestly, with all due love and respect, I'm annoyed by the mere thought of my past. Not because it was so bad but more so at the fact that I've allowed it to debilitate my process by endlessly engaging in the decapitation of me from my gift: the present juncture. So I vow, to forgive and accept my experiences, detaching myself from that non-existent negative space which doesn't encourage my positive evolution. I'm unable and unwilling to continue putting up with any thoughts, behaviors, or people that don't serve a higher, more undeniably favorable purpose in my life. My power lies in my ability to be sick and tired of being sick and tired.

March 2

Today I choose to be APOLOGETIC. I take full responsibility for the unenlightened wrongs I have committed against others and myself. I comprehend the effects of my actions and wholly validate the derived pain and truth. I aim to amend the injuries I have caused by identifying areas in myself that are in need of growth and healing so that I can make better choices in the present and the not so distant future. I bring to light the article of ignorance, insensitivity, insecurity or indiscipline that led me to err, and work to remediate it. My power lies in my ability to own the lesser parts of myself.

March 3

Today I choose to be A FULL COUNT. To say the least, this game of life and I have produced some harmfully unfavorable scenarios. As a result of my obstructed perception, my success and development have been severely delayed. I have been stuck in between the shadows of my yesterday, perpetually operating with my back against the wall. I always seemed to strike out at the most inopportune moments, leaving advantageous circumstances stranded in time space like runners on bases waiting to be driven home. However, visiting my past so often has shown me a new truth and I no longer have to push, pull, fight, or win because I've finally realized that the struggle is illusory! Regardless of how fragile I was in my past, I still manage to BE. My power lies in my ability to always take my best cut and swing for the fences.

March 4

Today I choose to be PAYING UP. With relief, I clean my slate by delivering what is owed to others. I make good on promises made, or otherwise seek forgiveness of remaining balances. I free myself of all self-induced obligations, giving thanks that I am able to help others prosper, cleansing myself of any negativity attached to my previous indebtedness. My power lies in my ability to reconcile my accounts on the material and ethereal planes.

March 5

Today I choose to be RETURNING HOME. I now realign with TRUTH after generations and lifetimes of separation. I recapture the Divine Knowledge that has been hidden, kept, or denied from me without sanction. I become enlightened as to the actual nature of my Highest Self. My power lies in my ability to claim that which is mine by Divine Right.

March 6

Today I choose to be HEALING. With my thoughts, I navigate every cell and energetic impulse toward my natural state of perfect health. I allow myself to let go of the pain and disease so that I may recapture the peace, prosperity, and wholeness that I am intended to possess. My mind and body overcome every setback as I lay claim to the condition of optimal wellness that is mine. My power lies in my ability to align with the Divine Intelligence that maintains me in full flourish.

March 7

Today I choose to be GRACIOUS. I AM congenially detached when I witness the mistakes, misgivings, or misfortunes of others. I aim to help those in my life maintain their dignity amidst undesirable circumstance, even though I perceive their role in the creation of such events. Pride is preserved in my presence. My power lies in my ability to be unimpressed by human error.

March 8

Today I choose to be MOVING FORWARD. I allow myself to make peace with my current circumstances and then proceed to channel my energy toward my next venture. I free myself by disregarding the idea of what could have been and embracing the possibility of what can be. I recognize that each stage of my life is built upon the completion of a previous phase. My power lies in my ability to continuously create.

March 9

Today I choose to be STREAMLINING. In order to draw more affluence and good into my life, I must make room for it. It is imperative that I free myself of negative people and behaviors if I am to receive the blessings that I seek. I show that I am ready to prosper by preparing my life for increased abundance. My power lies in my ability to recognize and eradicate energetic clutter.

March 10

Today I choose to EMBRACE FAILURE. If all my efforts resulted in success, I would be unable to learn and grow. I view my losses as a natural part of the life process that guides me toward better paths and approaches. I recognize that every experience can serve me in some way, if I allow them to. My power lies in my ability to distill lessons.

March 11

Today I choose to be SELECTIVE IN MEMORY. I benefit far more by dwelling on the positive aspects of a person or situation than by ruminating on the negative qualities. As I think of my life, I recall the most beautiful and meaningful events to savor and appreciate. I present my past in the best light possible. My power lies in my ability to narrate my story.

March 12

Today I choose to be WITHOUT JUDGMENT. I realize that external appearances are often inadequate or misrepresentative of deeper truths. I refuse to label others. I acknowledge that an individual's totality is far more complex than what I AM able to observe. My power lies in my ability to undermine my need to categorize people.

March 13

Today I choose to EMBRACE DIFFERENCES. My beliefs and values are my own and I refuse to impose them on others. I decline to judge, choosing instead to observe and learn. I am detached from others' actions and free of the desire to control them. My power lies in my ability to realize that I am a part of the diverse collective and that there are many individual truths.

March 14

Today I choose to LOVE MYSELF. I realize that I AM best able to serve others when I first nurture myself. I AM only able to give that which I already possess. I treat myself as well as I treat others. My power lies in my ability to recognize the value in me.

March 15

Today I choose to be IMPERFECT. Regardless of my perceived flaws, I am deserving of my heart's desires. I AM allowed to make mistakes. I AM allowed to be uncertain. I still have growth to attain, and I have not yet come into fruition. My power lies in my ability to accept myself exactly as I AM now.

March 16

Today I choose to be REDEMPTION. I've experienced a myriad of physically painful and emotionally heartbreaking situations. It simply took one fervently focused look into those eyes of mine and I immediately felt free from all immoral actions, delusional blunders, and hateful energies! I am my saving grace and I will be humbled forever by God's presence in my life. I have been saved and I refuse to take this opportunity for granted. I have chosen to align my eyes with my visions. In this life, there are plenty of paths I could travel but only one of those roads will lead me to my spiritually unified oneness. My power lies in my ability to back all of my decisions with assured affection, transparent truthfulness, and deistic design.

March 17

Today I choose to be VEGAN. No longer will my personal gain be an excuse to hurt another. I have decided that I have a responsibility to take care of others and myself. I am going to dedicate my energy toward saving, sustaining, and evolving this wonderful world we call home. At some point, we will recognize that we are all harmoniously breathing on the same wavelength. My power lies in my ability to abstain from unconscious thinking because I realize that no one is superior or inferior to anyone else, regardless of what life form the UNIVERSE decided to provide him or her with.

March 18

Today I choose to be REPARATION. I have made some decisions that did not serve my highest self. As a result, I've run smack into the unintended consequences that were attached to those actions. In retrospect, I can easily say what I could have done better, but hindsight would not be 20/20 without the raw experiences that exposed the wisdom needed for my growth. Instead of me feeling down in the dumps, depressed, and regretful of my past, I hold my head up high and make amends for any wrong doing, injustice, and/or injury I've caused others and myself. I will focus on making the most nondiscriminatory and unbiased choices because the aftermath will positively affect the masses. My power lies in my ability to know that whatever does not kill me will simply make me stronger.

March 19

Today I choose to be A REVISION. Upon further investigation, I can now see that what I initially forecasted my life to be does not totally align with my karmic debt. It's virtually impossible to account for all of the gaps created by the conscious hiatuses I've taken in previous moments. That being said, I will repetitively gift myself love in each present point in time because the wisdom that I was blessed to receive from my past experiences has taught me that my future is indeed unforeseen. My power lies in my ability to review, amend, and include what I feel are necessary corrections to elevate my journey to greater knowledge and understanding.

March 20

Today I choose to be DIVINE ORDER. I AM responsible for my actions and current place in life. I need to understand that I AM exactly where I need to be according to the Supreme Being. Regardless of how I personally feel about my present situation, there is a transcendental truth that my five senses won't be aware of 99% of the life that happens in and around me. I will no longer complain, belittle others or myself, or judge anything that I'm blessed enough to experience. My power lies in my ability to acquit myself of all mythical convictions and shift my focus toward the supernatural disposition that always yields the specific amount of wisdom needed for my growth.

March 21

Today I choose to be NOT GUILTY. I realize that although I've caused others and myself deep pain, the agony received due to my misdeed was warranted by a negative act that they committed at a prior time exposing the falseness, myth, and belief that VICTIMS exist. Due to my lack of purity, I was chosen to be the executioner. I now recognize the affliction felt by those I've misled and self. I embrace repentance because I am cognizant that this process ignites the repairing of my prior wrongdoings. My power lies in my ability to not only feel the misery of the people I have hurt but also in asking the Universe to abolish the actual negative trait responsible for their suffering.

March 22

Today I choose to LET GO. It's become second nature for me to hang onto pain and suffering. When happiness stands before me, my first inclination is to say, "It's too good to be true." This kind of consciousness is what prevents miracles from materializing in my life. It is humanly impossible for me to have a satisfying and surprisingly supernatural future if I'm constantly hanging onto an unhappy and cynical past. If I have any ambition to move forward and positively serve my highest self, it's a must that I release my negatively charged egotistical emotional wants, making room for the life I so desperately desire. My power lies in my ability to remove my pessimistically driven thoughts and replace them with new electrifying beliefs!

FORGIVENESS

REFLECTION:
1) Define forgiveness.
2) What/who haven't you forgiven self/others for?
3) What is the cost of harboring hurt? How does it help you?
4) What behavioral patterns do you notice when you do / don't forgive?
5) What emotions are you experiencing? If negative, what changes are needed to evolve?
6) Do any fears exist because of your lack of forgiving self/others?
7) What experiences would be granted to your life if you were less judgmental of self/others?

CHOOSE TO ACT:
1) Practice replacing judgments of self/others with compliments. Love begets love.
2) Practice being open to hope, faith, and trust. A closed heart can't receive love.
3) Practice replacing blame with granting a pardon for negative energy. This will reflect responsibility for your desired outcome. No need to be a casualty of circumstance.

SEASON 2

COURAGE & STRENGTH

<u>COURAGE</u>

March 23

Today I choose to THROW CAUTION TO THE WIND. I've watched myself create situations and scenarios that only exist inside of my mind. To make matters more interesting, I've allowed these non-tangible items to prevent me from BEING what it is I know I AM capable of. What sense does that really make? Do I not really desire what it is I say I want? What is the root cause of my procrastination? News flash: unless I'm stuck inside of some illusory protective shell, by deciding to breathe, I'm naturally taking a chance at failure, disdain/regret, and potentially death with every thought, word, or action I invest my energy into. This will serve to be factual whether I AM aware of this often overlooked TRUTH or not. I must remain cognizant that for as many things that could go wrong in life, just as many could go right! My power lies in my ability to repeatedly take great risks because regardless of what emotions I embrace in the physical form, I can't diminish my Divinity.

March 24

Today I choose to be THE PROOF OF THE PUDDING IS IN THE EATING. Through experience, I've developed a particular set of skills that will no longer allow me to solely accept someone else's word as my absolute truth. Living my life based on another person's beliefs would be inauthentic to my purpose. Call me old-fashioned, but I just don't believe in a cookie cutter way of being. I AM no robot and being programmed is not on my agenda. My power lies in my ability to always seek the true value and quality of all things during each and every way in which I am blessed to participate.

March 25

Today I choose to be EMBRACING THE UNKNOWN. I can only become secure by relinquishing the need for security. I trust the balance of the Universe, knowing that I AM protected by Divine Love. I acknowledge that magic is only possible by allowing for the occurrence of infinite possibilities. My power lies in my ability to release my need to control.

March 26

Today I choose to be YOU SNOOZE, YOU LOSE. In my world, all things happen just as they're supposed to...whether I like it or not. I refuse to regret any of my past decisions and/or experiences. I can't know what I don't know...so punishing myself further would make absolutely no sense whatsoever. In efforts to avoid future calamity and disappointment, I will BE aware and open to honest communication with myself first and foremost but with others also. Unlike the cocky Hare, I will emulate the Tortoise remaining loyal to my purposeful goals and steadfast throughout this journey because I AM convinced that losing was not made for me! My power lies in my ability to know that although good things come to those that wait, the early bird always catches the worm.

March 27

Today I choose to be A ROSE THAT GREW FROM CONCRETE. To say my life has been hard thus far would be putting it lightly, but heedless of how inhumane my surroundings were, I would always hear a voice saying, "EVERY DARK CLOUD HAS A SILVER LINING" and "JUST BECAUSE I AM IN THE WORLD DOESN'T MEAN I HAVE TO BE OF THIS WORLD." Oddly enough, I began to ask people "WHAT'S RIGHT?" As a substitute for asking "WHAT'S WRONG?" I became excessively optimistic, displaying my dogmatic faith because I know that I AM covered by an all-loving covenant. Due to the fact that I AM breathing this air and no one can legitimately tell me why, compels me to see the DIVINITY within myself and all other things. My power lies in my ability to know that regardless of where we're from, what we have, where we go, or what we do during this life, escaping death isn't optional; therefore, there is no reason valid enough for me not to BE what I AM, everywhere I stand!

March 28

Today I choose to be AN EYE FOR AN EYE. . I often dream of a conscious class of co-existing beings and how much smoother life would flow if our intuitive senses were once again common. There would be no room for jealousy, judgment, hate, poverty, or pain. Instead of inflicting hurt upon humanity, our first response would be lending a helping hand. Call me crazy, but I BELIEVE. My power lies in my ability to set the bar by being an example of honesty, displaying courageous acts backed by strong moral principles, and remaining undivided in TRUTH.

March 29

Today I choose to be WHEN PUSH COMES TO SHOVE. When the pressure is on, I will increase my willingness to endure what I've identified as a burden and allow my INTESTINAL FORTITUDE to lead me into the light of darkness. When the situation becomes critical and urgent, I will allow my PATIENCE to comfort me while I proactively develop solutions for my problems. When the time has come for action, I will effortlessly LEAD BY EXAMPLE simply due to the fact that I believe in myself. I have a backbone and my dogmatically diligent approach to consciousness has afforded me the privilege to live life, totally detached from time and fear. I do what I can, when I can, as best as I can. My power lies in my ability to prevent shit from hitting the fan by not allowing the subjectively significant stressful challenges of life to burst my mental pipes.

March 30

Today I choose to be A TUNNEL VISION. I have made a rigorous effort to eradicate any and all negative distractions from my subconscious mind. In order to assist myself with this seemingly tedious process, I chose to dissect and accept my role in my past. Doing so drastically improved the consolidation of my mental and physical efforts. I developed the capacity to enhance my visual exclusion, which allows my brain to ignore the non-essential information I AM met with throughout each day. I've learned that if IT isn't for me, naturally, against me IT is. This simple truth helps me remember that what's seemingly impossible today will be tomorrow's reality. My power lies in my ability to believe in the substance of things hoped for and the evidence of things not seen.

March 31

Today I choose to be AN OPTIMIST. The fact that just about everything I was exposed to as a youth pretty much showed me exactly what not to do, is irrelevant in the grander scheme of things because at the end of the day, I AM the only person responsible for me. Although my surroundings were the antithesis of affluence, I've decided to be disposed to only taking a favorable view of things. God is great and that Almighty source has convinced me to instill complete trust in all that I AM, but the streets were even better because they taught me COURAGE...the unyielding strength to ACT in the face of pain and grief! Regardless of what others aren't, I AM aware that every great achievement was once considered impossible. My power lies in my ability to know that when Fear knocks at my door, I need to answer it with FAITH.

April 1

Today I choose to be A GUNSLINGER. Whether it is in business, politics, or random charity, I will act aggressively and decisively because I know my intentions are ordered with the source of all moral authority. Although it may appear I take excessive risks and am seeking large gains to outsiders, my success comes through mindful observation and painstakingly time consuming inquiries that have solely been yielded from my experiences. Therefore, my nerves are un-rattled, my eye is steady, and my trigger finger is quick. My power lies in ability to know that my weapon of choice is and will always be derived from LOVE!

April 2

Today I choose to be INNOVATIVE. My methods for BEING are new, advanced, and original. My thinking will always go beyond what I can see because I desire to look beyond the obvious. Although the world may appear ordinary to most, I can feel the extraordinary in all things. I'm inspired to dig deeper and deeper into the core of my soul's existence, introducing fresh ideas and more ingenious schemes focused on ending the self-inflicted enslavement of our subconscious mind. Doing so will actualize the acceptance of our TRUE POTENTIAL, allowing us to live solely from a place of insightful understanding. My power lies in my ability to invent my own traditions.

April 3

Today I choose to be LAWLESS. I AM unrestrained by law, at times unruly, and I have never been a fan of the transmission of long-established customs and beliefs from generation to generation. That way of being promotes inherited, established, and customary patterns of thought, action, and behavior. I understand the basic principles of life will never change, but today's concepts and scenarios are drastically different. That being said, unless someone else can live life through my eyes and/or in my footsteps, I will converse with myself more and others less. My power lies in my ability to always dance to the beat of my own drum.

April 4

Today I choose to be AN EXPLORATION. I try new activities and ways of being without expectation of specific outcomes or purpose. I expand my knowledge of SELF by experiencing diverse modes of expression. I discover hidden talents and abilities by allowing myself to struggle, be uncomfortable, or fail. My power lies in my ability to embrace curiosity.

April 5

Today I choose to HAVE STANDARDS. I establish conditions that govern my decisions to expand energy or attention on people or projects. I express my respect for myself by refusing to participate in ventures or affiliations that don't reflect my TRUE WORTH. I recognize when I AM presented with an opportunity that will elude me from my PATH and willingly decline the offer. My power lies in my ability to value who I AM and what I have to offer.

April 6

Today I choose to DO WHAT I NEED TO DO. I strive every day to part ways with attitudes and habits that keep me from acting from my HIGHEST SELF. I acknowledge TRUTHS that challenge my present way of being. I open myself to change in ways that may be uncomfortable or unfamiliar to me. My power lies in my ability to make difficult decisions.

April 7

Today I choose to be WEIGHTLESS. I am unbound, unburdened, unblemished. I move through the world free of encumbrances and impediments. I easily increase my position, attaining higher and higher expressions of SELF. My power lies in my ability to release limiting beliefs.

April 8

Today I choose to be IN THE BELLY OF THE BEAST. I grew up in the heart of a danger zone. Each day was the equivalent to the front lines of war. Every decision deemed to be critically life-threatening. One could think of Detroit as being described as a place that solely provides residents with the most portentously formidable situations. In order to survive amongst the kingpins and hustlers who ran the neighborhood, I had to be like a cop working undercover infiltrating a mob family, being in that crucial position of having gained their trust and being a key part of its operations. My margin for error was nil and the only way I escaped was by always allowing my ALL KNOWING prime mover to guide my every resolution. My power lies in my ability to behold all of the abundance that surrounds me!

April 9

Today I choose to be EMPOWERED. By taking responsibility for my life, I unlock my inherent abilities to make change and progress. I claim my power, shedding any identification I have as a victim of martyr. I embrace the Divinity that flows through me, freeing myself of all perceptions of ineptness. My power lies in my ability to operate from essence and not ego.

April 10

Today I choose to DEFY THE ODDS. I create my own possibilities, probabilities, and statistics. My chances are as high as I expect them to be. Alleged facts and figures only apply to me if I accept that they do. My power lies in my ability to believe in myself above all.

April 11

Today I choose to be GOING FOR IT. I fearlessly pursue that which I desire most. Starting today, in this moment, I take action to draw forth to me my hopes and dreams. I allow my exhilaration for a coveted goal to carry me forward on a path of intent and resolve. My power lies in my ability to give myself permission to follow my heart.

April 12

Today I choose to be VULNERABLE. I willingly show my true nature to another, trusting that I will be accepted and warmly received. I expose my innermost Self in an effort to forge a deeper bond with someone who cares for me. I express my needs, fears, and hopes, revealing my most human modes of thought and desire. My power lies in my ability to garner the courage to let my guard down.

April 13

Today I choose to be FEELING SAFE. The Universe embraces me and helps me to succeed. Those I encounter facilitate my growth and well-being. I AM aligned with the Greater Good that permeates and flows through all things. I have nothing to fear. My power lies in my ability to relax and enjoy my blessed journey.

April 14

Today I choose to be LETTING GO OF EXCUSES. I acknowledge that there are more reasons why I can than why I cannot. The Universe is on my side and wants me to succeed. As I consider my dreams, I refuse to get caught up in my need to know how they will manifest, focusing instead on the fact that they are materializing now through my simple agreement to bring them into my experience. My power lies in my ability to allow good things to come into my life.

April 15

Today I choose to be ON FIRE. I AM an infinitely expansive material that generates a luminous warming affect. I AM able to create chemical reactions and alter my physical surrounding. My implications depend on whether I AM intentional and controlled or careless and untamed. My power lies in my ability to reach high states of energy.

April 16

Today I choose to be AUDACIOUS. I live fearlessly, fueled by my own belief in SELF. I dare to follow my dreams, refusing to pursue anything less than my greatest ambitions. I want victory, and I'm going after it! My power lies in my ability to unleash my inner warrior.

April 17

Today I choose to be USING MY WILL. I know my heart's desire, and I decide now to bring it into existence. I AM certain, determined, and unyielding. I AM a causal agent. My power lies in my ability to make solid decisions.

April 18

Today I choose to be CHANGE. I desire to be different, so I will do different things. I start my process of evolution now, with a singular, manageable step. As I persist in my efforts, my progress accrues, and a new ME emerges. My power lies in my ability to exercise choice.

April 19

Today I choose to be HAVING SELECTIVE HEARING. I realize that others' opinions are just that, opinions. When someone tells me that my aspirations are unworthy, impossible, or unrealistic, I know that their views are simply reflections of their own limited beliefs. I refuse to adopt the defeated perspectives that others allow themselves to accept. My power lies in my ability to disregard.

April 20

Today I choose to be TENDING TO MYSELF. Although I care about those around me, it is not my responsibility to provide them with solutions or handle their problems. I AM compassionate and empathetic, but I realize that each individual must learn his unique lessons in order to rise to his next level. I refuse to distract myself from my own need for growth by focusing on the plights of others. My power lies in my ability to create boundaries.

April 21

Today I choose to be EMBODYING MY ENDEAVOR. My thoughts, words, feelings, and actions are all aligned to my ultimate end. I AM one with my mission. I perpetuate my ambition with every expression, statement, and choice. I exemplify absolute congruence. My power lies in my ability to internalize, that which is to be externalized.

April 22

Today I choose to be FOCUSING ON WHAT'S IMPORTANT. There are many directions in which I can direct my energy, but only certain paths are worthy. My thoughts are too valuable to be indiscriminately dispersed. I attend solely to matters that foster my evolution and well-being. My power lies in my ability to be selective.

April 23

Today I choose to be AMBITIOUS. I AM highly motivated to achieve my goals. I refuse to allow obstacles to deter me from my pursuit of success. I AM driven from my innermost point of consciousness. My power lies in my ability to be energized by my desires.

April 24

Today I choose to be LIVING BY FAITH. I acknowledge that what I AM able to decipher with my five senses is only part of the story. I know that my desires precipitate first in the spiritual realm before taking on physical form. I affirm that the Universe has my best interest in mind and that all things are possible. My power lies in my ability to believe.

April 25

Today I choose to be SETTING THE BAR. I live life by my own standards and create my own definition of success. I determine who I AM and where I AM going. I do not look to others to validate my choices, nor do I expect them to feel, think, or act as I do. My power lies in my ability to stand alone.

April 26

Today I choose to be A RISK-TAKER. I embrace challenges, realizing that they are an important part of my story. I act in FAITH, having full belief that my choices lead to the rewards I seek. I live my life without self-imposed limitations, and I appreciate struggle as an element of progress. My power lies in my ability to claim my destiny and move courageously toward it.

April 27

Today I choose to be REFUSING TO BE A PRISONER OF HABIT. I recognize that my freedom lies in my option to choose new behaviors and methodologies. I fearlessly embrace growth and change. I see potential to create a new SELF through the process of initiating new actions and ways of being. My power lies in my ability to not allow my fear of the unknown to stand in the way of my intentions.

April 28

Today I choose to be A FLAG. I fly high, holding tight regardless of how hard the wind blows. I may be shifted from side to side but I will never be blown down. I stand by my values and others look to me as a symbol of character and consciousness. My power lies in my ability to be proud of my convictions, steadfast in my beliefs, and certain of my integrity.

April 29

Today I choose to be MONDAY. I AM full of potential and I set the barometer for what is possible in the days to come. I AM a torchbearer, leading by example, building dynamic energy that carries over to those that follow me. I may not be as popular as others, but I know that my role is important, and I recognize my unique purpose. My power lies in my ability to command respect with my presence by ceaselessly serving to solicit everyone's best efforts.

April 30

Today I choose to be A SPIRITUAL AGENT. I know without pondering, believe without seeing, and accomplish without doing. I live by my faith, my consciousness, and my inherent power to manifest my desires. I AM perpetually cognizant of my connection to that which is all-powerful and understand that with my intentional congruence to my source, all is possible. My power lies in my ability to know that all the answers and solutions I need are located within me.

May 1

Today I choose to be PROVIDENCE. I make a conscious effort each moment to mimic God's activity while I AM in this world. The Most High has always kept me in its protective care. I will be forever grateful and accepting of the higher power that resides in and around me. Due to its inextinguishable perennial presence, I AM now submissive to TRUTH, only allowing the LIGHT to guide my every move. My power lies in my ability to diminish the role of fear and become thankful for all things in life always knowing that I AM protected by the Divine Superintendent.

May 2

Today I choose to be A SHOT IN THE DARK. I AM aware that others will judge me simply because of the way I look and where I was born. None of which really matters in the grand scheme of things. My whole life, I've heard what I can't do and where I can't go, but to be totally honest, it never felt like they were referring to me. My vision may not be clear to others and that is perfectly fine by me. As long as I understand what I AM, I will always be cognizant of what I can do. I have been blessed with the ability to see with my conscious mind and not the limited images that my eyes deceivingly portray. My power lies in my ability to know that I can't base what I'm going to be off of what everyone else isn't.

May 3

Today I choose to be THE MIRACLE CURE. I AM inexplicable by scientific laws and most consider me to be Divine. The only reason my welcome is so surprising to the masses is because they are governed by the almighty egocentric flesh. I often hear how highly improbable and overwhelmingly challenging it can be to live a conscious life but contrary to that belief, just as much, if not more energy goes into living unconsciously. Whether I AM busy with vigorous action or operating dormant, I still remain motivated to BE...I CAN'T NOT be what I AM! All things are derived in my MIND and I have the authority to reign supreme over my internal filtration system. My power lies in my ability to dig deeper curing the cause and not to simply remedy the effects.

May 4

Today I choose to be A CATALYST FOR CHANGE. I AM the substance responsible for causing the events and situations in my life to sway one way or another. Only I, not others, will be the reason I behave the way I do. I am the stimulus that provoke the general desire and willingness to do whatever it is I decide to do. My power lies in my ability to ignite my spirit galvanizing the verves and muscles needed to materialize my unforeseen dreams.

May 5

Today I choose to be ONCE IN A LIFETIME. Life does not allow us to replay any past events. Each moment will only happen once. Therefore, I will not rush any decisions because time is of the essence. I'm aware that I have little to no control of when that time will expire. I will not allow death to be the catalyst of my thoughts and actions. Instead, I will properly plan a program geared towards my soul's premeditated purpose and methodically execute my proposed objectives to their fullest, one step at a time. My power lies in my ability to know that when I combine PREPARATION with OPPORTUNITY, the end result will be very unusually prosperous and extraordinarily special.

May 6

Today I choose to BE. I AM moral excellence, goodness, and righteousness representing all human hospitality, kindness, and passion. I AM here because a small degree of hope was sufficient enough to cause my birth. Even if the staggering statistics of my soul's field of all potentiality is too much for my ego to mentally grasp and physically accept, there are just as many scientific facts backing my spiritual wealth. So with this opportunity known to most as life, I will choose to be ALIVE! My power lies in my ability to know that I can run but I can't hide...simply because I AM!

May 7

Today I choose to be GROWTH. In spite of the declared difficulty and opposition, I'm continuing to work firmly and obstinately while on my quest to elevate SELF. My intense focus during this process has allotted me the opportunity to increase not only my material size, but also my spiritual strength. Now that I'm physically developing and mentally maturing, I AM in a position to share my gifts with my community so that we can become better citizens of the world! My power lies in my ability to create habitual behaviors that are aligned with my spiritual purpose.

May 8

Today I choose to be DETERMINATION. I will establish my goals and dissect several possible routes to achieve them by carefully researching and intuitively guiding my calculations. This process will ensure purposeful actions are exceeded with a firmness of passion and resoluteness. My destination of desire will be short lived by design because of my relentless ambitious pursuit of what is rightfully mine. I conclude that there is only one path to failure, by allowing an absence of genuine grit and perseverance to outweigh my will to succeed! My power lies in my ability to drive further even when the effort appears to be painful.

May 9

Today I choose to LIVE OUTSIDE OF DOMESTICATION. Until now, I spent my life locked up in the system. I allowed my parents, siblings, neighborhood, church, and government dictate what MY life should be. I held myself accountable to those unrealistically strict standards and heavily judged myself when I failed to meet them. I told myself "I'M NOT GOOD ENOUGH" and often asked, "WHAT IS WRONG WITH ME?" The fact of the matter is, no one is superior/inferior to anyone else. I have MY own dreams, MY own goals, and this is MY life. My power lies in my ability to realize that the purpose of life is to live life with purpose.

May 10

Today I choose to be SPACE AND TIME. I've mistakenly felt that rewards are not the results of good deeds, punishment is not attached to evil actions, and life lacks legitimate lawfulness. Unfortunately, I've overlooked the fact that TIME is the distance between cause and effect. The perceived coincidences and random events that occur in my life are merely the delayed effects of my previous positive/negative actions. Therefore, I need to realize that every thought, action, and word count toward the yielding of consequences or dividends will come back to me in full measure. My power lies in my ability to transform my present, by allowing the wisdom gained through past experiences to assist me with assuring my purpose filled future.

May 11

Today I choose to be RELEASING. It's been extremely difficult for me to let go of yesterday becoming enslaved to my past. I've made it second nature to hang onto agony and affliction. I feel that I want to be happy but whenever something good occurs in my life, I say, "ITS TOO GOOD TO BE TRUE." I am solely responsible for preventing my joy-filled future from manifesting. I need to stop being doubtful as to whether something worthwhile will happen to me and be more trusting. My power lies in my ability to become undoubtedly optimistic remembering that the source of my fulfillment, also known as the Universe, is all loving, divinely intelligent, and infinitely abundant.

May 12

Today I choose to be THE ANNIHILATION OF AFFLICTION. I've attempted to run and hide from my true problems using my external addictions as an alleged shield. The faster I ran, the bigger the initial complication became. The dilemma was that my puzzling predicament was predicated on my cowardice perception of reality as opposed to positively asserting FAITH in my Higher Source. My power lies in my ability to conceptualize the fact that everything will be ok in the end and if it's not ok, it's not the end.

May 13

Today I choose to be A CHILD. Whenever you see me, I will be proudly wearing a smile on my face and having fun. I will explore the world, I will not be afraid to play, and never will I be scared to express what I feel. Furthermore, I will not worry about my past nor will I care much about the future. Instead, living in the present moment will dominate my focus. My power lies in my ability to rid myself of the alleged need to please others, to be accepted by others, and in turn will live life to please ME!

May 14

Today I choose to be THE ART OF TRANSFORMATION. I will achieve this mastery of change by refining the fear-based agreements that presently make me suffer. I will reprogram my own mind as opposed to accepting society's cookie cutter style of living. Exploring and adopting alternative beliefs will yield the possibility of ending the emotional pain I've endured opening the door for me to enjoy my life and begin new dreams. My power lies in my ability to break the habits that limit my growth, which will allow me to gain more personal power and become stronger.

May 15

Today I choose to be THE GREAT ESCAPE. I'm tired of being a hostage to the constant pressure to outdo friends, family, and colleagues. Being in bondage to my reactive impulses and self-absorbed desires are no longer acceptable. I hate that I've become a prisoner to other people's perceptions of me and incarcerated by the need for their acceptance. There is no better time than NOW for me to break the shackles of my ego because it is only good for giving me the illusion that I'm acting freely…when in reality, I've remained captive to its hoggish appetite. My power lies in my ability to get away from externally based character flaws, selfish inclinations, and the "ME ONLY" mentality.

May 16

Today I choose to be DEFYING GRAVITY. My true destiny is to obtain control of all reality through the force of my imagination. The power of my thoughts will be guided by the Light within my soul. I will look beyond the illusions that I've created and allow the authentic yearnings of my heart to be my primary motivating force in life. My power lies in my ability to unleash the functions of MIND over MATTER, eliminating the control over me by the visible world becoming the true captain of my own fate.

May 17

Today I choose to be DIALING GOD. There are many negative forces that attempt to block and impede my prayers while traveling through the spiritual network. Although I've gotten busy signals, experienced static on the line, and at times, gotten cut off when I dialed up, I refuse to stop praying. Instead of continuing to create more negative forces with my behavior and unkind words, I treat all things with deep respect, adoration, and love. Without a shadow of a doubt, I know the LIGHT is always there, never changing, and forever willing and able to fulfill my every desire! My power lies in my ability to acknowledge that I am responsible for getting my prayers answered.

COURAGE

REFLECTION:
1) Define courage.
2) How does your fear help you survive? Where does it debilitate you?
3) What "path" in your life is worth your deepest passion, time, energy, and effort? Why?
4) Where are you most / least courageous?
5) Where do you not give yourself credit for your courage?

CHOOSE TO ACT:
1) Practice embracing failure. By default, there's always a silver lining.
2) Practice following your intuition. It's your voice of reason.
3) Practice being creative. Adversity is the genesis of creation.

__STRENGTH__

May 18

Today I choose to be A SURVIVOR. I have been through incredible lows in my life but I AM still here. There have been points that were so dark that I could not see a way out but I have found light. Regardless of how I have been labeled, attacked, or betrayed, I know who I AM and I AM resilient. My power lies in my ability to trust my vision of myself and my faith in the future.

May 19

Today I choose to be THE BREAKING POINT. Now that I'm at the point at which my physical, mental, and emotional strength has given way to stress, what am I to do next? Now that my seemingly tangible conditions and situations that encompass my life have become critical...who am I to call on? I AM aware that a change is needed but where am I supposed to start? Although it may appear that I've lost everything I know and love, in retrospect, that couldn't be further from my absolute truth. In essence, I've helped myself create an opportunity for growth. I've subconsciously suppressed my negatively charged egotistical habitual ways, ridding myself of all things that don't serve my HIGHER standard for BEING. My slate is clean, my vision is clear, and I can see that my daunting past simply created favorable circumstances in this present moment. My power lies in my ability to know that the embodiment of my experiences in their entirety, were merely trials of the loyalty of my TRUE beliefs and I will never collapse under pressure.

May 20

Today I choose to be NEW HEIGHTS. Just because something sounds hard doesn't mean that it's going to be. Removing the external stress and pressure from my way of being, has encouraged me to stop limiting myself to the boundaries of my comfort zone. I no longer box my thoughts and I refuse to hide from my greatness. I will hold myself accountable by developing a schedule that makes the best use of my time; one that addresses my strengths, weaknesses, imbalances, and areas for opportunity without any of the fluff. My power lies in my ability to create a mindset that will push me past my normal work-intensity, while servicing my well-being.

May 21

Today I choose to LEAD BY EXAMPLE. I've learned that when others attack me, it's never because of what I AM even if the verbal assault(s) appear to be personal. I'm cognitively aware that life is a creative art. Generating more guerilla warfare by responding to their negatively charged commotion with more hit-and-run tactics, would only fuel their fire. I will select the words and actions that yield the utmost love and tender care. I have become addicted to taking responsibility and ownership of all things I experience in my life by ceaselessly being the prototype of what I desire. My power lies in my ability to know that if I don't take control of my mind, it most assuredly will take control of me.

May 22

Today I choose to be ABLE. I can do what I AM setting out to do. I AM capable, competent, and committed. I AM encouraged to face any task through the knowledge of my TRUE SELF and my consciousness of the abundance of the Universe. My power lies in my ability to get out of my own way.

May 23

Today I choose to be DRESSING FOR THE OCCASION. I robe myself in FAITH, TRUTH, and creative empowerment in service of unequivocal triumph. I conquer fear, doubt, and lack with a suit of optimism, trust, and gratefulness. Clad in enlightened attitudes and Divine Love, I AM prepared to overcome all challenges and obstacles. My power lies in my ability to wield the armor of Spirit as my first line of defense.

May 24

Today I choose to be DELIVERING. I make good on promises, intentions, and claims. I AM good at what I do and my results speak for themselves. I show rather than tell. My power lies in my ability to manifest tangible milestones.

May 25

Today I choose to be WILLING. I genuinely entertain new ideas and possibilities. I AM open to change. I agree to suspend my values and beliefs for the time being so that I may fully absorb the opportunities for growth that are available to me NOW. My power lies in my ability to consent to the process of my own evolutions.

May 26

Today I choose to HAVE STRUCTURE. I plan time and activities to foster mental, physical, and spiritual growth. I create systems that bode well for my success in a defined goal or desire. I organize my life to allow for clarity of thought, purpose, and action. My power lies in my ability to impose form and function on time and space.

May 27

Today I choose to FEEL. I recognize that although some emotions are uncomfortable or even painful, I must honor them in order to return to my desired equilibrium. By fully experiencing my feelings, I open the channels through which any related negative energy can be released. I find solace not by suppressing my emotional signals but by allowing them to manifest to fruition without resistance. My power lies in my ability to respect all aspects of my Human Nature.

May 28

Today I choose to RECOVER. Though I have become wounded, injured, or ill, I AM on the rebound to perfect health. For any misfortune I encounter, I know that a return to Divine Equilibrium will follow. I AM getting better, stronger, and more whole. My power lies in my ability to affirm total wellness as my natural state of being.

May 29

Today I choose to GROW. I enlist the wisdom gained from prior experiences to guide the decisions I make now. The choices I make provide evidence of my evolution. My deeds demonstrate my increased degree of consciousness. I AM led to believe that my future Self will be proud the person I AM today. My power lies in my ability to transmit a higher vibration in my thoughts, feelings, and actions.

May 30

Today I choose to GO ABOVE AND BEYOND. I view the minimum as a starting point. I seek to provide service that far exceeds what is expected. I allow love to dictate the amount of effort I AM willing to put forth. My power lies in my ability to give unconditionally.

May 31

Today I choose to be PREVENTATIVE. I take preemptive actions to avoid undesired events. I practice my wisdom regularly in order to build my immunity and ward off depression, insecurity, and disease. My positivity hygiene is outstanding! My power lies in my ability to consistently and continually develop my physical, spiritual, and emotional wellness.

June 1

Today I choose to be IMPACTFUL. I unequivocally affect those around me by inspiring them to evolve and thrive. I AM a catalyst for change as I speak words of encouragement and possibility to those who seek my counsel. I see the light in others and I draw it forth. My power lies in my ability to recognize my capacity to influence.

June 2

Today I choose to SWIM. With every stroke, I get closer to my destination. Even though the water may be cold, deep, or shark-infested, I AM determined to reach the shoreline. I realize that treading water will only waste my energy and further alienate me from my goal. My power lies in my ability to persist.

June 3

Today I choose to TAKE ACTION. I will not get overwhelmed by the amount of things that need to be done but instead will focus only on the great work that I can do right now! I realize there is a time for thinking and a time for implementing my intentions. Any angst I feel in regards to the road ahead is dissipated through the process of taking steps on that very road. My power lies in my ability to be proactive.

June 4

Today I choose to PROTECT MY JOY. I refuse to pollute my energy by being indiscriminate about the company I keep. I recognize how far I've come and will defend my continued evolution from any force that aspires to disrupt it. I AM immune to others' attempts to spread their own dissatisfaction and misery. My power lies in my ability to lovingly release those who no longer serve me.

June 5

Today I choose to EXCEL. I embrace the fact that I stand out. I AM great at what I do and I AM recognized for it. I exceed expectations, climbing as high as I choose to go. My power lies in my ability to maximize my talents.

June 6

Today I choose to PERSEVERE. Regardless of the challenges I face, I continue on my chosen path. I endure hardships by operating from my point of intention and by turning obstacles into opportunities. I AM committed to my mission and relentless in my belief in myself. I AM immune to conditions and convinced of my capacity to succeed. My power lies in my ability to actualize my goals and my refusal to allow circumstances to dictate my determination.

June 7

Today I choose to be A CHAIN-LINK. I AM part of something bigger than myself, eternally connected to my fellow beings. I AM aware of how my actions affect others and how we are all able to serve or sabotage each other. I honor my role in this conglomerate, striving to better my brethren as I better myself. My power lies in my ability to find strength in my unity with others.

June 8

Today I choose to SEE NO EVIL, HEAR NO EVIL, and SPEAK NO EVIL. I won't allow negative imagery to disturb my vision, negative thoughts to enter my mind, or negative words to come out of my mouth. I refuse to dwell on undesirable possibilities, nourishing only concepts that serve me holistically. My power lies in my ability to embody serenity and a life that flows with peace and positivity.

June 9

Today I choose to be AN EQUINOX. I AM the epitome of evenness. Day and night have approximately equal lengths. My movements are closely monitored but never are they made short work of. Although the road has already been paved for me, I must establish my own line of travel and I refuse to take short cuts. Time is relative and hurriedness is never allowed. I have two ears and one mouth...so it would only make sense for me to listen at least twice as much as I talk. My power lies in my ability to create stability between my carefully formulated thoughts as well as my deliberately planned external locomotion.

June 10

Today I choose to be LOGISTICS. This world, with the help of my actions, has at times presented me with some pretty complex situations. When searching for comfort, the mirror was the last place I desired to look. Especially when you consider that I was at the forefront of my turmoil. However, I will not feel sorry for myself and I refuse to be a victim of circumstance. I will make conscious efforts to create detailed plans focused on organizing my objectives and specifying my solutions. When done to scale, the results will be nothing short of engineered genius. My power lies in my ability to increase the awareness of my perceptions, beliefs, and attitude by viewing negative reactions and feelings of disempowerment as indications for the need to further understand my own thinking.

June 11

Today I choose to be IMPREGNABLE. Some would say that I have been to hell and back but regardless of how tragic my past experiences have been, my FAITH remains unable to be defeated or destroyed. I create more positive chains of events by remaining hopeful and confident about my future. My optimistic approach to life has helped me develop a system of BEING that can't be broken by doubt, negativity, or stress. My power lies in my ability to realize that no matter how long the shock lasted as the result of my emotionally disturbing experiences, I AM still breathing and my purpose will continue to be fulfilled.

June 12

Today I choose to be MOVING ON. I've found myself looking for reasons to stay with people, yet for that very reason should have been more than enough for me to leave. Sometimes displaying strength means being able to cry, yet remain steadfast with each step along my path. Regardless of the circumstances, I must be strong enough to let go. I refuse to waste my time looking back at what I've allegedly lost because life was not meant to be traveled backwards. My power lies in my ability to know that at some point along this journey of mine – people, places, things, or ideas responsible for my present pain did not live in my world and then, like now, I AM just fine!

June 13

Today I choose to be ICE WATER VEINS. Pressure can only be perceived and even if I believed in it, I would still remain cool. Getting rattled is totally out of the question for me. I will remain calm and in control of myself. My deeply rooted tireless faith is never in question or doubt because it is backed by a higher source. My power lies in my ability to master the two C's: CONCENTRATION and COMPOSURE!

June 14

Today I choose to be INDEFATIGABLE. In spite of difficulties, obstacles, or discouragement, all that I AM and all that I do consist of steady persistence and is backed by purpose. My mode of operation is synonymous with steadfastness. I align each thought I think with tenacity focused solely on the manifestation of my soul's aspirations. Each step along my journey is accompanied by a continuance of grace to the end leading me to my eternal salvation. My power lies in my ability to mimic diligence, dedication, and immovability because these qualities are essential to success.

June 15

Today I choose to be AN ACT OF VALOR. I AM unconcerned with the way people perceive me, and how they feel I should react during times of crisis. My strength of mind enables me to encounter danger with firmness and personal bravery. The unyielding burning desire that my spirit is blessed with, has always supplied me with the adequate amount of backbone needed during the dire straits of life's many lessons. I love the self-induced electrifying feeling of being daring enough to follow my intuition in all that I do heedless of what those around me may say or do. My power lies in my ability to dance to the beat of my own drum!

June 16

Today I choose to be AN ORGASM. I AM the climactic result of patience, deliberate intent, dedication, tenacity, and perseverance! I'm always at the height of happiness and establishing an everlasting aura of ecstasy is what I'm best known for. I'm the light at the end of the tunnel...the pot of gold at the end of the rainbow...and the calm after the storm! My power lies in my ability to remain steadfast knowing that my backbreaking labor-intensive journey will lead me to eternal euphoria!

June 17

Today I choose to be A WARRIOR. I will rebel against the invasion of parasites that attempt to control my brain. Just because I've declared war, doesn't guarantee a victory in my favor. I proclaim that always achieving my best is my only logical option because "doing" so, will at least provide me with an opportunity to be free. My power lies in my ability to choose the highest possible path yielding at the very least, the dignity of rebellion.

June 18

Today I choose to RECAPTURE THE SPARK. My negative actions have created negative effects. I have found myself stuck in what feel like first gear, my energy reserves are on empty, and my life force has slowly been sapped! Each reaction created a new negative force that has robbed me of my SPIRITUAL LIGHT. Despite the fact that I'm at a point of desperation, these dark entities have no life of their own...they solely survive off my energy. I will be a prisoner of darkness no more. My power lies in my ability to NO LONGER nourish actions derived from selfishness, intolerance, anger, fear, or any other REACTIVE trait.

June 19

Today I choose to be LOGICAL. My thoughts and actions are governed by principles of proof and inference. I'm pleased with my current state of being while refusing to allow myself to be deliriously happy, overlooking the process that led me to my NOW. I am calm, focused on attending the needs of my best interest. My power lies in my ability to compartmentalize my feelings relying on data and facts.

STRENGTH

REFLECTION:
1) Define strength.
2) What is your biggest fear? What is the impact it has on you by allowing it to conquer you?
3) If attaching expectations of self and others to the outcome wasn't available, how would you create your future?
4) What are your strengths/weaknesses?
5) What is the cost (negative effects) of you not applying your strength?
6) When the fear of failure appears too massive to bear, what steps do you take to overcome?

CHOOSE TO ACT:
1) Practice living from passion. Life is all fun and games from there.
2) Practice going against the grain, from love. Bet on self and risk taking the unconventional route to your destiny.
3) Practice acting from a place when you've felt advantageous in life. Give yourself an opportunity to succeed.

SEASON 3

HONESTY & LOYALTY

<u>HONESTY</u>

June 20

Today I choose to be HONEST. I refuse to deny or omit matters of fact for the sake of exploiting situations. I take ownership of my Lower Self's follies and failings. I speak Truth even when it is uncomfortable or unprecedented. My power lies in my ability to be transparent.

June 21

Today I choose to be STRAIGHT AND NARROW. The way of proper and honest behavior is the quickest path to eternal happiness. When conduct is aligned with integrity, drama burden, and anxiety are naturally released. The world was built to develop character. Setbacks and deep distress helps propel life forward. When everything seems to be going against me, I will emulate airplanes because they take off against the wind, not with it. My power lies in my ability to know that life is a series of experiences; each one makes me better.

June 22

Today I choose to be AN OPEN BOOK. My life has been filled with a maze of mysteries. My intricately complex design, coupled with the divisional contrast between mom vs. dad, right vs. wrong, and spiritual vs. physical, led me down a dark path full of both unintentional and deliberately false statements. I devoted my time, efforts, and energy into poisonous pits of self-pity, wallowing in my pool of sorrow, only to discover that I was deepening the disconnection from the one source that could set me FREE. I've learned that heedless of what my external distractions may be, I have an alliance to self. I will live a life derived from enlightened fulfillment by honoring the validity of my reality. My power lies in my ability to liberate myself from deceit and distortion by allowing access to sincere TRUTH to reside in my heart.

June 23

Today I choose to be THE HORIZON. This is the point of the story where I look myself in the mirror and accept responsibility by taking ownership of my mind, body, and soul. I'm immediately relieved of any stress, anger, and disappointment. My carcass becomes overwhelmed with an abundance of gratitude, humility, and unrestricted love. My soul's focus is now my sole focus. I am now a living, walking epiphany! My mind has stopped thinking and I KNOW and FEEL beyond an intellectual logic. My power lies in my ability to always display open and honest communication with others and myself.

June 24

Today I choose to be YOUTHFUL. I vibrate a frequency of health, virtue, and effervescence. I'm at my prime, conquering the horizons of today, excited about the many wonderful days that lie ahead. With fresh perspectives, an open heart, and an unchained spirit, I brighten the world. My power lies in my ability to live passionately.

June 25

Today I choose to be BEAUTIFUL. I am a unique expression of Divine Splendor. I radiate my internal loveliness to the world. All that I say, think, and do is aesthetically pleasing. My power lies in my ability to embellish and enhance the greater community.

June 26

Today I choose to be AN ARCHETYPE. I represent a set of Higher Values. I AM a Universal symbol that resonates with the good in everyone. I AM the stuff of myths and legends. My power lies in my ability to be known for my character.

June 27

Today I choose to SILENCE MY INNER CRITIC. I recognize that negative perspectives about me only serve to deter me from my true capacity and worth. I quickly dismiss derogatory thoughts as they arise, refusing to be my own worst enemy. I encourage, appreciate, and motivate myself through positive observations and unconditional love. My power lies in my ability to censor my intrapersonal dialogue.

June 28

Today I choose to DISCLOSE MY AGENDA. I AM straightforward in my intentions and forthcoming in my motives. I AM candid with my objectives as my foremost desire is to achieve that which is in the Higher Interest of all involved. I refuse to manipulate, deceive, force or mislead as I go about getting what I want. My power lies in my ability to lead and live through transparency.

June 29

Today I choose to be WELL-CONNECTED. My bonds with others are solid, balanced, and authentic. I engage wholeheartedly with my friends and fiduciaries, having chosen them with consciousness and care. I bring my healthiest self into the lives of others knowing that any internal issues I have will become magnified under the illumination of relationship. My power lies in my ability to give of myself openly and honestly.

June 30

Today I choose to be SUBMISSIVE. I yield to the mysterious ways of the Universe, relinquishing my need to control processes and outcomes. I defer to the knowledge of my Higher Self, turning from the fear-based pleadings of my ego. I allow my natural good to come to me rather than struggling to create false impressions of prosperity. My power lies in my ability to distinguish Truth from illusion.

July 1

Today I choose to be SPECIFIC. I know exactly what I want. I have a precise vision of that which I desire. I have considered in detail the form, function and features of the object of my pursuit. My power lies in my ability to clearly communicate to the Universe the TRUE yearnings of my heart.

July 2

Today I choose to be CONGRUENT. My personal truths are apparent in my every expression and manifestation. My actions are in harmony with my values. My beliefs are my own and I take responsibility for them. My power lies in my ability to recognize and reconcile discrepancies in my philosophical platform.

July 3

Today I choose to PERCIEVE REALITY AS A MIRROR. My thoughts and attitudes are reflected back to me by my external world. My own beliefs actualize before me in physical replica. By observing my experiences, I AM enlightened to the images and ideas that I project. My power lies in my ability to recognize my reflection when I see it.

July 4

Today I choose to SPEAK MY MIND. I express my thoughts and feelings, refusing to repress the energy they possess. I acknowledge that my beliefs and perspectives have value. I honor myself by allowing my TRUTH to be known. My power lies in my ability to gain respect through being heard.

July 5

Today I choose to be A CRITICAL THINKER. I carefully consider ideologies that are presented to me before adopting or rejecting them. I AM not easily convinced and generally unaffected by the surface-level presentation of events and personalities. I seek deeper, more thorough understandings of theories, beliefs, and choices. My power lies in my ability to assess.

July 6

Today I choose to be TRANSPARENT. I have nothing to hide, so I hide nothing. My actions are congruent with my statements. I AM genuine with my intentions. I attract unguarded relationships by displaying trustworthiness, and trusting in the goodness of others. My power lies in my ability to self-disclose.

July 7

Today I choose to be EPIC. I AM greatness personified. I exemplify the utmost parameters of love and beauty. I AM an expression of Supreme Being. My power lies in my ability to maximize my perception of myself.

July 8

Today I choose to BE A PEACE OF MIND. I realize that bouts of happiness or anguish as a result of a fleeting experience will inevitably be fleeting, however I can decide to be at peace at all times. How I perceive situations determines how I feel about them. Meaning is not found within an event itself but in how I frame the event. My power lies in my ability to reconfigure my emotional interpretations.

July 9

Today I choose to be PRISTINE. I AM cleansed of all negative influences, past and present. I AM pure and immaculate-untouched, unmarred, unscarred. I AM purged of all resentments, fears, untruths, and self-defeating concepts. My power lies in my ability to mentally, emotionally, and spiritually keep house.

July 10

Today I choose to be AUTHENTIC. I refuse to adopt attitudes, values, or ways of being simply for the benefit of others. I AM absolved of societal expectations and unconcerned with making impressions. I wholly value the attributes that have been granted to me and I express myself accordingly. My power lies in my ability to own my truth.

July 11

Today I choose to HONOR MYSELF. I recognize that I AM intrinsically valuable and deserving of my heart's desires. I contribute great things to the world by expressing my unique gifts. My aspirations are worthwhile and my beliefs are relevant. I consistently draw to myself that which reflects my regal nature. My power lies in my ability to respect my own divinity.

July 12

Today I choose to MAINTAIN MY INTEGRITY. My values and actions are consistent and I do what I say I will. I honor myself by staying true to what I believe. I do not allow others' attitudes to influence my principles. My power lies in my ability to be authentic.

July 13

Today I choose to be ASKING. I know what I want and I invite it to manifest now. I AM always in the process of receiving, as I AM fearless in expressing my desires. I speak my request and believe that it is coming to me as I await its physical precipitation. My power lies in my ability to make my needs known.

July 14

Today I choose to LOOK INSIDE MYSELF. I recognize that all that I desire originates from within me. I can provide the answers that I seek. Only I know what's best for me. My power lies in my ability to trust myself.

July 15

Today I choose to be FATUOUS. Throughout my life, I have been foolish and frivolous with my time, money, body, and ideology. I have unconsciously allowed the outside world to prescribe me with a formula for failure. My mind-set has become so narrow that I've somehow coerced myself into believing that the TRUTH is something that actually causes me pain. Ceasing this constrictive way of thinking will eliminate the complacent illusory manner in which my subconscious mind has been conditioned. My power lies in my ability to know that it's extremely difficult for the blind to lead the blind.

July 16

Today I choose to be THE AXIOM. I AM the genesis of all things. Although my abstractly defined structure has yet to prove the legitimacy of solidarity, my existence in ALL is an undeniable TRUTH. The validity of my absoluteness is beyond doubt and has been established from birth. If ALL things are created with the presence of a ceaselessly flaming fervor, the only logical conclusion for me is to accept the actualization of my abundantly authentic self-evident ascendancy. My power lies in my ability to know that regardless of what something may currently appear to be, the intended inception of its individuality was derived from LOVE!

July 17

Today I choose to be THE TRUTH. I desire to model my life in accordance with fact and reality. In all that I can mentally conjure, verbalize, and physically execute, there will lay genuineness, faithfulness, and objectiveness. In order for my life to be in the absence of erroneous falsehoods, I will to practice the acceptance of all things as they are. My power lies in my ability to seize each moment as a possibility to be present and honest, first and foremost with SELF, endlessly engraving my allegiance deeper and deeper between the powers that be.

July 18

Today I choose to be REVEALING THE CONCEALED. Like a SEED buried in the ground before producing a tree or a baby sheltered in the womb before being born into our world, my creations have been harbored in my mind long enough. The time is now for my harvest to produce. All things from the genuine LIGHT of the Universe to the ultimate truths of life are first hidden prior to being discovered. It's up to me to strive to uncover these truths, to restore the BRILLIANCE into the world so that pain, suffering, deceit, and hatred are eternally destroyed from the landscape of human existence. My power lies in my ability to bring forth the powers of observation to see the truth and the courage to handle it.

July 19

Today I choose to REMOVE HATRED. Human behavior and the human heart are the sole determining factors as to what occurs in our environment. All destruction, including what we perceive to be natural disasters, materializes for one reason, which is our prejudice toward our fellow beings. Whether my explanation(s) appear to be valid or invalid, whether I'm aware of it or I'm in self-denial, harboring even the slightest bit of hatred or animosity for another person will still bring destruction to the world. By cleansing the hatred in my own heart, I can remedy all the world's problems at the level of their root cause. My power lies in my ability to be painfully honest, acknowledging every person or group of people toward whom I feel anger, envy, malice, total disgust, or any combinations thereof and approach them all with intense feelings of deep affection.

July 20

Today I choose to be FULL-STRENGTH. I proffer my convictions and beliefs with the utmost potency. I express myself in true, undiluted terms, honoring my values and way of being amidst a sea of alternative approaches to life. Refusing to water-down my ethical platform for the sake of impressions, I take pride in whom and what I AM. My power lies in my ability to be totally committed to my core beliefs.

July 21

Today I choose to be WEIGHTLESS. I refuse to continue to allow others the ability to bring me down. Just because we are in the same space does not obligate me to be affected by their negative gravitational attractions. Stress, affliction, and fear have no place in my atmosphere because those wasted emotions only lead to everlasting entanglement. My power lies in my ability to make unbiased decisions relieving me of all mental bondage.

HONESTY

REFLECTION:
1) Define honesty.
2) How are the areas you're not being honest about related to acceptance, forgiveness, courage, and strength?
3) What are you most/least honest about? Why?
4) What are your determining factors for being honest?
5) How does being honest make your life more/less difficult?
6) What role does integrity serve in your life?
7) In what ways does your relationship to respect for self/others dictate your choice to be honest?

CHOOSE TO ACT:
1) Practice not making the same mistakes twice. Truthful behavior must first be applied to and with self.
2) Practice using honesty as a tool to encourage self/others.
3) Practice simplicity. Only share what happened; not your desired outcome.

<u>LOYALTY</u>

July 22

Today I choose to be LOYALTY. I always hear that "YOU'RE ONLY HUMAN" when things don't appear to go according to plan as if being human is an excuse for me to accept being less than what I AM. The truth of the matter is, I AM not just HUMAN...I'm also a BEING and Earth is not my final destination. I'm cool with the vulnerability, but I refuse to accept mediocrity selling myself short of my DIVINE ONENESS. I have created a strong feeling of support between my external body and my internal self. My intricately designed systems were made to flow in unison. My power lies in my ability to know that FAITH without WORK is dead.

July 23

Today I choose to be A PRISONER OF WAR. I've witnessed the most sanctified Christians become dedicated to spreading the word of Jesus Christ; yet they forget to abstain from judging and condemning the alleged sinners they're attempting to save. I've also seen heartless killers so devoted to being ruthless, they lose their souls in the process of ruling the underworld, decide to live by the gun and therefore, die by that same notion. Regardless of who we are or where we're from, we all have a vice in this seemingly tangible world. No two people are going to see life through the same lens, which means, no one is right and no one is wrong. For that reason, I will be indefatigable in my approach to be what I AM; everlastingly remaining unwilling to accept the adaptation to intimate association with human beings. My power lies in my ability accept me for me, creating a single-minded loyalty for my inner brilliance, and permanently refraining from being a victim of circumstance.

July 24

Today I choose to STAY IN MY OWN LANE. Regardless of how much I display acts of idolatry, blasphemy, deception, and/or jealousy, I can't change or escape myself. I can only live the life that I AM in. I will mind my own business. I will continue moving straight ahead without attaching the need to allow other people's perspectives and behaviors to veer over into my personal affairs. I have been blessed with life and whether I succeed, fail, or what have you, that's up to me to decide. At the end of the day, I AM solely responsible for me, nothing more and nothing less. My power lies in my ability to focus on being in the driver seat of my own life in the absence of back seat drivers.

July 25

Today I choose to be POETRY IN MOTION. My thoughts are intentionally strung together with a purpose of graceful fluidity. The movement of my actions are accompanied with tactful elegance throughout. This enlightened way of being is all possible due to the fact that I never fight myself. I willingly help, selflessly support, and endlessly encourage me to BE my very best at all times, heedless of the outcomes or circumstances. Doing so allows me to develop a sublime relationship with myself. My power lies in my ability to know that although I am not without flaw, I AM perfect just as I AM.

July 26

Today I choose to be CONCENTRATION. Even if I didn't possess a keen awareness to what is taking place in and around me, life doesn't start or stop moving simply based on my reserved perspective of reality. My physical facts of existence are merely reflections of the actions I took while previously focusing my intentness towards those specific cerebral images in the past, independent of the depths of my mental efforts. I will start dealing with one particular thing above all others, being whatever I deem to be most important in my life at the time. I can't control others, but I CAN always be cognizant of what is. My power lies in my ability to know that I don't have enough time, knowledge, or currency to not pay attention.

July 27

Today I choose to be MY BIG BREAK. I've always heard that little becomes much and all journeys start with a single step. To be honest, until NOW, it all appeared to be fluff to me. What I've come to realize is that, it was to me what I perceived it to be. Every moment assisted the grand re-opening of my mind, and as a result more opportunities have been allotted to me. It's like my accomplishments are leading me to more accomplishments. My power lies in my ability to know that regardless of how much I abstain from vanity and boastfulness, I will never limit myself or lower my own importance…I AM the fuel to my FIRE!

July 28

Today I choose to be THE HUMAN STRUGGLE. I realize that the root cause of our collective limiting beliefs can be located in the inability to understand the vastness of space and all that's in and around it. When I remove myself from myself and BE who I truly AM, GOD, I can then feel the plentiful power bestowed upon me. Whether or not I comprehend what I'm proclaiming, accepting circumstance, or paying attention to surroundings, I understand that the cause of suffering as well as the solution to all of my problems start and end with the essence of me! My power lies in my ability to not focus on the fictional egocentric fairy tales, and live through the God in ME.

July 29

Today I choose to ROLL OUT THE RED CARPET. No longer will I accept being anything less than what I AM. I've grown to know that I AM a person of great importance and I deserve the utmost respect, love, and adoration. If I AM to be given anything in this life, I desire for it to be treatment befitting royalty. I AM aware that my decision making may have at times appeared to be mistakes in the eyes of others but I recognize that they were simply another way of doing things. So I AM and will continue to be proud of what and who I AM because no other person was special enough to be chosen to play the role of ME! My power lies in my ability to not only be cognizant of the rules of life, but also to be conscious that I AM the only exception.

July 30

Today I choose to be SELF POSSESSED. I have a divinely intelligent mind, an infinitely abundant brain, and a fully functional body. Why would I ever elect and adopt the lifestyle that others suggest I follow? I'm not saying that I'm not appreciative of all the assistance I receive; I'm simply suggesting that I must first understand what and why I desire the things I do. Once I'm cognizant of those things which are essential for my growth, I can then legitimately request the aide from others. I trust in my ability to discern, and will ask myself what I need most. In order to ensure that I obtain these necessities, I will develop a plan of action focused on doing what's in my absolute best interest. My power lies in my ability to obtain full command of my faculties, feelings, and behavior.

July 31

Today I choose to be A KEEPER. I take care of those in my circle, doing what I can to provide them with love and guidance while allowing them to learn the lessons that are necessary for their evolution. I lookout for the welfare of those closest to me, expressing my TRUTH in the form of concern, input, or feedback without casting judgment or assuming omniscience. I take it upon myself to help others stay on track with their Higher Selves by speaking the right words at the right time. My power lies in my ability to advocate for others' well-being.

August 1

Today I choose to be LOVED. I graciously receive other's gifts or material and ethereal goods. I bask in verbal and physical affirmations of my value in this world. I joyfully acknowledge the time and service that is selflessly given to me by my closest companions. My power lies in my ability to recognize the many ways in which affection is expressed.

August 2

Today I choose to be A HUMANITARIAN. I contribute to the progress of the human race by bettering myself and serving others to the best of my ability. I proffer guidance and positivity to the network that is already available to me, creating ripples of love that expand outward to the greater community. I realize that I can make significant contributions to the world, wherever and however I AM. My power lies in my ability to care creatively.

August 3

Today I choose to be STILL. I don't take action. I don't make effort. I don't struggle. I don't strive. I relinquish in totality to the most peaceful state of being I can access. As I release my focus on external activity, previously unattended to emotions, energy, and insights rise to the surface of consciousness and guide me gently toward higher degrees of enlightenment. My power lies in my ability to build a close relationship with MYSELF

August 4

Today I choose to be VALIDATION. I fully give attention and consideration to the beliefs, opinions, or ideas of others. I express my respect for another's perception of circumstances, though it may differ from mine. I make my best attempt to understand an alternative view, suspending my own position for the moment. I acknowledge individual realities and truths, affirming their value and relevance. My power lies in my ability to listen actively.

August 5

Today I choose to be MULTICULTURAL. I embrace the diverse ways in which I live and express myself. I recognize that the food I eat, the clothes I wear, the language I use, the media I consume, and the people I love originate from a multitude of places, periods, and paths. I AM under the influence of infinite orientations to life. My power lies in my ability to perceive the ways in which I AM inexplicably intertwined with others.

August 6

Today I choose to be A HOST. I graciously welcome others into my personal world. I AM hospitable and attentive, enthusiastically anticipating the needs of those I receive. I provide a sense of comfort and belonging to those I care about. My power lies in my ability to put others at ease.

August 7

Today I choose to CREATE HAPPINESS. I realize that my optimal state of being is not something that happens upon me but rather something that is self-generated. I become untroubled by following my passion and aligning with my purpose. My power lies in my ability to evoke feeling by being then doing.

August 8

Today I choose to be MY OWN BEST FRIEND. I continually
see the best in myself, through the highs and lows. I AM always
there, armed with unconditional positive regard. I treat myself
with care, kindness, and appreciation and take the time to enjoy
my own company and attend to my own needs. My power lies
in my ability to love myself.

August 9

Today I choose to be FULLY COMMITTED. I AM willing to give an unlimited amount of myself in order to achieve the results I seek. I AM solely devoted to that which is most important to me. I AM not fazed by the choices or actions of others and I AM unaffected by any obstacles I encounter. My power lies in my ability to be resolute in my decision to invest.

August 10

Today I choose to be RANDOM ACTS OF KINDNESS. Now and forever, I will perform selfless acts to either help or cheer up strangers. For no special reason, aside from attempting to make others happy will serve as my primary source of stimuli. My actions will be spontaneous or planned in advance but either way, they will be encouraged by my omnipotent universal life force. My power lies in my ability to remember that the gifts rendered to me were not meant to be hoarded, but instead, shared with my spiritual brothers and sisters.

August 11

Today I choose to be INTIMACY. My soul has been dying to build a close familiarized friendship with my body. It desires to create a private and cozy atmosphere. The foundation of this relationship will not be rocked easily because it is derived from love, affection, mutual respect, and passion. This union will play a central role in my overall human experience, serving my need to belong and to love another. My power lies in my ability to give credit where and when credit is due.

August 12

Today I choose to be COMPASSIONATE. I AM compelled to improve conditions for those who are physically or spiritually impoverished. I see the positive contributions I can make in the lives of others and am moved to give of myself by an inner sense of duty. I AM keenly aware of the Oneness that exist among all Beings. My power lies in my ability to make a difference.

August 13

Today I choose to be A FRIEND. I encourage, inspire, and uplift those around me. I share my positivity with all I encounter. I AM an ally and a supporter. My power lies in my ability to extend myself to others.

August 14

Today I choose to be NO AGENDA. I plan to befriend others with the absence of hidden schemes. I will perform favors with zero strings attached. My friendships will lack self-interest and ulterior motives...in return, true and loving friends, joy, and fulfillment will be attracted into my life. My power lies in my ability to derive pleasure from the unconditional anonymous act of pure sharing, expecting nothing in return.

August 15

Today I choose to be ACQUIRING A SILENT PARTNER. No matter what circumstances I find myself in, I know that my positivity is there to help me get through it. I AM never alone. I have access to unlimited assistance and support; all I need to do is rely on my faith. My power lies in my ability to team with my Higher Self.

August 16

Today I choose to be A LOCOMOTION. There are many types of trains depending on where they're running and what they carry. Upon further investigation, I AM much the same. I used to feel burdened and bogged down by what I perceived to be excessive loads. I felt that my experiences were so traumatic; I wouldn't have wished them on my worst enemies. At times, I was moving so slow; it felt as if I was barely moving at all. I have been on these tracks for a while and I now realize that I've housed precious cargo safely moving it from point A to point B. Doing so has allowed me to inspire, empower, and enhance myself and others in ways that were previously deemed inconceivable during this journey. In retrospect, slow motion is always better than no motion. My power lies in my ability to thank God for making me what I AM because no one else could fill these shoes of mine.

August 17

Today I choose to be PRIORTIZING. I will first determine the order for dealing with my series of tasks according to their relative importance. Once I designate each assignment systematically from first to last concern, my focus will be keen and I won't move to the next project until the one I'm currently working on is complete. Through my experiences, I've learned that MULTI-TASKING is just another word for starting a lot and finishing very little. My power lies in my ability to set precedence over my life making sure that my needs come before my wants.

August 18

Today I choose to be COMMITMENT. My goals and I will be bound together like Siamese twins. I deserve to obligate myself to every step of the systematic series of actions directed toward my desired end results. Nothing will be deemed more important than whatever it takes in order for me to inspire my highest self at all times. Each instant will be devoted to following my inner voice and I will remain faithful for the duration of that premeditated time period. Achieving the greatness I know was intended for me is not optional...IT'S THE ONLY LOGICAL SOLUTION. My power lies in my ability to enjoy every moment of every second of the process because without it, there would be no "dream come true".

August 19

Today I choose to be FLOURINSHING. I will make bold statements followed by extravagant gestures flowing in the direction of my purpose in life. I will grow spiritually developing a healthy mind and body in each and every moment. My brandish actions will mirror my prosperous thoughts. For I AM the epitome of working toward a common cause through cooperative and coordinated efforts that are concentrated on the best interest of my god-like materialized corpse. My power lies in my ability to prepare myself for greatness thriving on every opportunity my daily experiences provide.

August 20

Today I choose to be APOTHEOSIS. I have been elevated to divine status and my life has been deified. However, with great power comes great responsibility. Therefore, the remainder of my physical existence will solely be of a benevolent nature. I will continue to show a deep respect for all living and non-living things, because we were all created in the likeness of the altruistic, celestial Supreme Being. My power lies in my ability to know that chivalry is indeed alive and I'm encouraged to give freely, only backing it by assured affection.

August 21

Today I choose to be THE HUMAN BODY. All by myself, I AM my own universe. I possess thirteen major organ systems, seventy-eight organs, two hundred six bones, two hundred ten distinct cell types, between six hundred fifty six and eight hundred fifty muscles (depending on the source), and approximately fifty trillion cells! Each system functions involuntarily independent of each other while simultaneously working together systematically to keep me alive and active. Every living organism in my body plays a specific role related to my health and development. As you can see, my body is a lot like life. Although I have my own spiritual purpose and physical agenda, there still remains the need to collaborate with others and myself in order to manifest the change I desire to see in the world. My power lies in my ability to know that like an astronaut viewing Earth from the vastness of space suddenly realizing, my views on life are forever changed and it becomes clear that what matters most is to protect this place that bears so much LOVE in it, fostering the very root of life!

August 22

Today I choose to be DEEP AFFECTION. Whether I AM
being referred to as an interpersonal attraction, a romantic love,
sexual pleasure, or familiar fondness, I only represents human
kindness, compassion, and adoration for all. The 'I AM' in ME
is benevolent and loyal as it pertains to the concern I have for
the good of another. I AM the happy feet that guide your swift
and free dance moves…the gap between your thoughts…and
the wind beneath your wings. My power lies in my ability to
remember that there is no place here for the possessive clutch,
the clinging arm, or the heavy hand.

August 23

Today I choose to be SELF-PRESERVATION. I've spent the bulk of my life living according to the subjective standards of family, church, and society, but now it's time for me to get back to my original state of being. Down to my fingerprints, I'm different and perfect just the way I AM. I accept my strengths as well as my perceived flaws. I AM this way because I AM supposed to be and there is absolutely nothing wrong with that. My natural instinctive tendency is to protect myself from harm...so why does my life consist of so much pain? My power lies in my ability to rely on my innate desire to remain ALIVE in my own life regardless of my past decisions, my current circumstances, or my future mishaps.

August 24

Today I choose to be GIVING & TAKING. I will practice and master the art of compromise. The success of any partnership heavily depends upon the implementation of balance. I will have conversations throughout the day with myself and others that reflect the lively exchange of positive ideas. Although my perspectives may differ from time to time, the fundamental principles in which they stand will not. Remaining humble and grounded in my faith promotes discipline, structure, and detains my focus on being familiarized with favorable end results. My power lies in my ability to uncannily bend but not break.

August 25

Today I choose to be A COLLABORATION. I will repeatedly take the action of working with my spirit and body so that I can produce and create a life derived of euphoric nirvana. My efforts to align forces will consist of a series of intellectual, unprejudiced, and equitable decisions. Those choices will allow me to make peace within, take empowering actions, and exceed my wildest expectations! My power lies in my ability to DO WHAT I LOVE, and LOVE WHAT I DO!

August 26

Today I choose to be A PARENT. I will share my teachings and tools with humanity as if it was my child. I've been deemed responsible for the upbringing of my children in the world, but I must remember that they are not mine. They are instead, a gift given to me from the Universe. This opportunity gives me a chance to share, grow, and to become a kinder, more tolerant person. I'm more aware of my ability to be and spread the LIGHT. I will practice what I preach, becoming an embodiment of strength. My power lies in my ability to lovingly, respectfully, and selflessly share all of the wisdom I possess with my children by SHINING through in all of my actions.

August 27

Today I choose to be TEAMWORK. I AM the combined action of a group of people that yields effective and efficient results. Keys to successful alliances include communication, coordination, mutual support, effort, cohesion, and balance of contributions. Due to the fact that "WE" can get more accomplished collectively than "I" can alone, I will suppress my ego from a place of love. I will dedicate my efforts to coming together for the overall common purposes and goals, which will subordinate the need of my individual desire to stand out. Talent may win games, active participation, a joint effort, and intelligence wins championships! My power lies in my ability to know that TOGETHER, EVERYONE ACHIEVES MORE.

LOYALTY

REFLECTION:
1) Define loyalty.
2) Where in life are you disloyal and don't show up for self? Where does that leave you?
3) How balanced are the loyalties in your life with regards to self, family, work, and friends?
4) What are your determining factors for being loyal?
5) How does being loyal make your life more/less difficult?
6) What value does intimacy, connection, and trust hold for you?
7) In what ways does your relationship to respect for self/others dictate your choice to be loyal?

CHOOSE TO ACT:
1) Practice trusting self and believe in your ability to be supportive, open-minded, and compassionate.
2) Practice taking into account the long-term repercussions of short-term rewards.
3) Practice giving firm and constant support to others and self. Create allegiance by being a person of high regard.

SEASON 4

CONCIOUS AWARENESS &
WIDSOM

CONSCIOUS AWARENESS

August 28

Today I choose to be CONSCIOUS AWARENESS. If knowing is half of the battle, what does the other half consist of? What is the point of having faith, but no work? Why can't I ever truly be FREE unless I've first forgiven others and myself? Well, I've learned that the answers to all of these simplistic complexities are one in the same. Newton answered it best when he defined his First Law of Motion. It can be stated as, "An object at rest remains at rest unless acted upon by a force. An object in motion remains in motion, and at a constant velocity, unless acted upon by a force." That being said, I need to be the catalyst behind my cognizance. My power lies in my ability to know that potential without action ain't shit.

August 29

Today I choose to be in a CLUTTER FREE ZONE. I will establish the specific areas of my life that I purposely desire to improve. After my deliberately intended scope of focus is identified, I will work until I've cleared out the rubbish. This process will be ignited by me asking myself, "What here is absolutely essential to my BEING?" I will then create homes for all of my necessary items and trash or give away the rest. I will remind myself where and why I made compartments for all things and always put them back in those spots. Doing so will coerce my new way of existing into habit-forming ways. I will remain cognizant of keeping this area clean so that I won't allow any sneaky hodgepodge to mess up my hard work. My power lies in my ability to remove the non-important items and people from my life, be vigilant in my approach to keeping it clear, and continue expanding my consciousness becoming fully enlightened.

August 30

Today I choose to be the sum of PREPARATION + OPPORTUNITY. Some like to refer to me as good luck. However, I'm simply playing my part by controlling the few things I can and not losing any sleep over the things, people, or situations I can't control. Each day, I ask myself, "WHAT DO I WANT NOW vs. WHAT I DESIRE TO OBTAIN LATER." Each thought I think, word I speak, and action I perform are accompanied by; "IS THIS DECISION HELPING OR HURTING ME?" I have absolutely no craving to hinder my forward motion, so I'll continue making strides to lean toward resolutions that aide the progress of others and myself. Doing so keeps me readily available for any and all scenarios presented in my space. My power lies in my ability to know that my success or failure is not only brought to me by chance, but rather through my own process of being.

August 31

Today I choose to be HANGING ONTO MY HOPES. I can create any and every excuse in the book but none of them will ever actually support my originally intended purpose. I could allow the fear of the unknown hold me back, but when have I ever truly possessed the ability to predict my future? Yet, I still EXIST! I've also noticed that talking alone doesn't propel me as efficiently or effectively as my actions. So my approach to life each and every moment will be backed with a lionhearted means of arriving from point A to point B. My past has taught me that I AM most comfortable when I am uncomfortable. Even the serious situations that are suspended by hair-thin strings excite me. My power lies in my ability to know that just because my dreams are out of sight does not have to mean they're also out of mind.

September 1

Today I choose to embrace that TIMING IS EVERYTHING. The UNIVERSE has a specific plan for my life and when I allow IT to be my guide, I AM never led astray. I will be calm and accommodating, allowing the DIVINE BEING to open my doors. Sure, I may have to knock...I may have to put forth some effort...but I've learned that rushing the process hardly ever works in my favor. I AM a believer in being aggressively assertive when pursuing the life of my dreams, but I will never FORCE anything. When I maintain my composure, allowing and accepting all things as they ARE, the HOLY SPIRIT has a way of making sure my ego, as well as my essence is pleased. So it's a win/win! My power lies in my ability to invest my energy into an unyielding, yet patient faith.

September 2

Today I choose to be THE BUILDING BLOCKS OF MOTIVATION. I must develop a general desire and willingness to do or be what it is I say I AM fascinated by. It's imperative that my decision making be heavily supported with logical reasoning and intentional design. Becoming an adept manager of risks will prove to serve as a viable skill set during this process...especially considering each and every assertion of belief I conclude will either lead me closer to my purpose for action or further away. If I legitimately have a longing to aspire to live a life fulfilled, I need not ever be indecisive because that is one of the quickest ways to stunt my spiritual, physical, emotional, and psychological growth! My power lies in my ability to not attempt to put the wrong picture in the right frame.

September 3

Today I choose to be MORE THAN WHAT MEETS THE EYE. Life for me has appeared to be more complex and difficult than what I previously deemed necessary. But who am I to dictate what's essential for growth, as if no one outside of me exists? The fact of the matter as I perceive it to be is that all events happen in DIVINE ORDER. That being the case, I'll trust my THIRD EYE, knowing that it has never, nor will it lead me, to places solely filled with pandemonium unless they were a part of the process that leads to my perennial paradise. I've learned that during times of darkness, my focus is keener, which encourages my vision to be most clear. My power lies in my ability to know that SEEING with my eyes is more DECEIVING than it is BELIEVING.

September 4

Today I choose to be a SERVANT LEADER. I've learned that obtaining power by way of force is not sustainable long-term and the fall from grace is never worth the price of fame. For that reason, the outdated, fear-based, top of the pyramid way of governing needs to be immediately abolished. Alternately, the wealth should be shared, putting the needs of the people first, and helping one another develop and perform as highly as possible. Doing so would coerce the enjoyment of peace, tranquility, and for lack of a better term, heaven on Earth! My power lies in my ability to know that ultimately, takers lose and givers win.

September 5

Today I choose to be PLUGGED IN. Dreaming of my future and dwelling in my past are two things I refuse to do. This present moment is all I will ever truly have and doing either of the aforementioned notions will leave me high and dry. I will prevent the feeling of sadness and displeasure caused by the nonfulfillment of my hopes and expectations of others by solely focusing on my own journey and purpose for being. I'd rather suffer from the pain of discipline than be disillusioned by what someone else failed to do or be for me. What I must remember is that they too, are traveling up a creek without a paddle. My power lies in my ability to think and listen at least twice before I speak because I AM aware that the intention behind my words have the power to influence success or failure in the consciousness of others and myself.

September 6

Today I choose to be THE KNOWER. I ceaselessly seek and acquire knowledge through my physical feelings of animate being and spiritual senses. I AM the subject constantly focusing my concentration toward a particular object. I AM the beholder continually aiming my deliberate intent on that which is being perceived. There is power contained in the act of holding my mind's undivided attention on an external/internal object or happening, whether it is my breathing, my thought flows, my whole-body presence, these words, a candle, or a sunset. I AM the journey as well as the destination. My power lies in my ability to remain aware of the KNOWN...the perceptual inputs from outside realities that I AM getting to understand better through my subjective interpretations.

September 7

Today I choose to be THE POWER OF ATTENTION. I've learned how to stay aware of my breathing regardless of the task at hand. I've learned how to expand my awareness to include my whole body in the present moment. In order for me to be alive in my own life, I need to dedicate myself to discovering more ways to target my heart's center, to love myself and those around me without judgment, and to open up to the flow of spiritual love and insight into mind, body, and soul. My power lies in my ability to master the art of being conscious of the perceptual inputs happening inside and around me that ground me in the immediacy of the NOW!

September 8

Today I choose to be A RESOURCEFUL PLANNER. I will create detailed proposals that are aligned with my goals. The future as it will BE is impossible to predict. However, my scheme will be designed with every possible specific aspect I can positively attract from the SUPERNATURAL. I have absolutely no need to ever hold back. I will give it my all, always, in all ways! My power lies in my ability to know that proper preparation prevents piss poor performances.

September 9

Today I choose to be A PROTOTYPE. I set the example for Higher Living by setting steep standards for self. I demonstrate proactive consciousness through integrity, congruence, and ownership of responsibilities. My way of being is hallmarked by selfless giving and unconditional love. My power lies in my ability to practice what I preach.

September 10

Today I choose to be SELF-MADE. I pursue my most authentic Self and in so doing find the path that fits me precisely. I create a life of my design through the universal resources that are perpetually available to me. I count blessings by doing all I can to elevate myself. My power lies in my ability to realize how powerful and perfect I AM.

September 11

Today I choose to be RUSSIAN ROULETTE. My mere existence is risk-taking within itself. This life will continue to be action packed and full of chance. I know that regardless of my TRUE intentions, towing the line and not saying all that IS, can be just as catastrophic as pulling that trigger. No one can read my mind. I'm going to be upfront and honest at all times...even when I don't feel that others are worth my time. This life I live is about my spiritual journey and not necessarily my role in theirs. I have a responsibility to the earth, the universe, and most importantly, to myself. As I go through each day, I may never know which spin of the cylinder will prove to be lethal but what I do know is that I will no longer decrease my odds of winning by increasing my lead for losing. My power lies in my ability to know that with every whirl of the wheel, I can be just as dead as I AM alive.

September 12

Today I choose to be AN ALCHEMIST. I seek to convert base materials into precious treasures. I affirm eternal life, as I pursue increasingly deeper understandings of spiritual health and evolution. I perpetually strive toward the highest version of myself and in so doing elevate the vibration of the world around me. My power lies in my ability to transform.

September 13

Today I choose to LISTEN TO MY INTERNAL VOICE. I validate the subtle messages that I intuit and in so doing quest deeper into the wisdom of my Higher Consciousness. I feel in my body when choices or situations are out of alignment with my Greater Good, knowing that I AM the best barometer of what is right for me. I experience the feelings and energies of others, sensing my way to greater understandings of individuals and dynamics. My power lies in my ability to allow my Divine Insight to help me.

September 14

Today I choose to be RECALIBRATION. I take time to assess the negative experiences and undue influences that have affected my outlooks on life and gently direct myself back to center. I take stock of my perceptions and release any beliefs that no longer serve me. I evaluate the degree to which my way of thinking resonates with my higher Wisdom and make adjustments accordingly. My power lies in my ability to recognize my own biases.

September 15

Today I choose to be GROUNDED. I AM present. My energy is concentrated and I Am focused. I feel firmly rooted in my earthly environment, as I know who I AM and what my purpose is. My mind, body and spirit are seamlessly and cohesively integrated. My power lies in my ability to create my niche.

September 16

Today I choose to be PARANORMAL. I exist beyond the comprehension of common science. My ways may only be explained by quantum calculations or Divine Insight. I know no bounds or limitations. My power lies in my ability to allow myself to be misunderstood by others.

September 17

Today I choose to be ETERNAL. The impact I make in this realm lives on indefinitely, as I do. I AM remembered in the minds of those both dear and unknown. My positive vibrations emanate to the ethers and beyond, forever echoing through the halls of infinity. My power lies in my ability to recognize that I exist, foremost, as energy.

September 18

Today I choose to be TRANSLATING. I guide others by working with them at their own level. I help make sense of Higher Concepts by packaging them in down-to-earth approaches to life. I use concrete examples to demonstrate Universal Principles at work. My power lies in my ability to disseminate knowledge in a way that resonates with others.

September 19

Today I choose to be KEEPING MY HOUSE IN ORDER. I take time to complete any unfinished business for the sake of streamlining my psyche and environment. I organize the extensions of myself so that they are easily and readily accessible when needed. I address the areas of my life that are chaotic, confusing, or complex, working to restore solace, certainty and simplicity. My power lies in my ability to be totally prepared for my next level of evolution.

September 20

Today I choose to be IN THE ZONE. My current state of consciousness has allowed my actual skills to match my perceived performance requirements perfectly in all that I do. It can be implied that my focus has increased and the attention I give to the action I'm taking concedes for higher levels of achievement. I AM operating in a machine-like optimal execution mode. My power lies in my ability to intuitively feel how the events in my life will unfold, creating the best possible behavioral state of being, focusing outward, trusting my physical motor responses, and doing things as if my life depended on it but staying aware of the fact that it doesn't.

September 21

Today I choose to be THE MYSTERY WITHIN. If I continue searching outside of myself, I will never discover my inner peace. There is an extremely exuberant amount of unexplainable supernatural power that lies beneath my body's surface and I AM the only person that can tap into it for me. Although my metaphysical curiosity has been aroused often, until now, this unknown FORCE has been kept secret from my subconscious mind. It took some time and I endured some unpleasant experiences but it was all a part of the process that led to me uncovering the conundrum of my intimate intelligence. My power lies in my ability to not only become more observant of the things that create disturbances inside of my psyche but also in replacing them with more empowering beliefs.

September 22

Today I choose to be HAPPINESS. Too often I've confused temporary pleasure with enduring enjoyment. It is necessary for me to remain focused on pleasing myself because the world and its negative capabilities can be potent and highly seductive. My wishes will be based on my needs and not emerged from the selfish external side of nature. My power lies in my ability to create the strength to restrain egotistical longings, specifically ask the Universe for what my souls needs, and the courage to develop a deep appreciation for whatever life brings me.

September 23

Today I choose to RECOGNIZE THE DESIGN BENEATH THE DISORDER. There are no coincidences, no chance encounters, and no random surprises in this game of life. Whatever happens, happens for a reason. When I react negatively to the apparently sudden chaos of life, I also deny the underlying purpose of CREATION. My attitude prolongs the madness and not that of others. The moment I recognize and accept the perceived hardships and all chaotic circumstances as opportunities for spiritual elevation, pain and doubt disappear. My power lies in my ability to comprehend that for every action, there is an equal and opposite reaction.

September 24

Today I choose to be LONG-RANGE VISION. My life has been full of heartache and problems mainly because I've failed to really 'SEE' the situations that confronted me. Due to my lack of ability to identify the long-term consequences of short-term decisions, I have had a tendency toward misjudgment. My miscalculated steps have led me to believe that I now possess the power of clear vision and foresight in every part of my life removing my blindfolds. My power lies in my ability to grasp the cause-effect relationship that governs all reality which yields the fact that my life choices and actions are motivated by ultimate results...NOT MOMENTARY ILLUSIONS!

September 25

Today I choose to be THE BUTTERFLY EFFECT. I AM the only person on the face of this Earth that can play the role of ME. No one else is equipped with the divinely unique skill set I possess. Although my localized changes may appear to be minute and lack significance to anyone outside of SELF, I'm reminded daily that I'm an essential part of this complex system and my input will have large effects elsewhere. I will seize each moment as an opportunity to be great. I can and will make each thought I think purposeful, each word I speak lovingly reverent, and each action I commit mindful of the spiritual well-being of others, myself, and the Universe as a whole. My power lies in my ability to know that even the greatest discoveries and inventions are merely collections of individual energies.

September 26

Today I choose to BREATHE. I take time to experience the life force that flows through me at this very moment. I inhale fresh, cleansing energy and exhale tension, negativity, and fear. I dwell on the cusp of body and spirit, appreciating the interplay between the physical and the ethereal. My power lies in my ability to be still.

September 27

Today I choose to be MY MOMENT OF TRUTH. I pledge to fearlessly honor my highest self at all times, acknowledging that the limiting beliefs I've created in my past were counterfeit. Following the guidance of my own voice, I will also have to occasionally endure brief time periods of isolation. I AM and will always BE all that I need me to BE exactly when it's required of me! My power lies in my ability to solely channel my energy toward the miracle of life and all that it encompasses right here and now.

September 28

Today I choose to be the EQUILIBRIUM. I balance the various aspects of my life in such a way that I feel centered and stable. My lifestyle provides for my mental, physical, and spiritual nourishment. I have outlets for my most innate drives, applications for my most prized talents, and opportunities to indulge in my most savored pleasures. My power lies in my ability to proactively tend to both responsibility and recreation.

September 29

Today I choose to MULTIPLY. Whatever I give returns to me in greater and grander quantities. All that I AM grateful for increases and expands. I experience more of whatever I focus my attention on. My power lies in my ability to transmit that which I desire to attract.

September 30

Today I choose to be UNDERCOVER. I move through the world without fanfare, spreading good in subtle, anonymous ways. I privately broadcast love to the world-at-large, silently channeling light onto everyone I encounter. I send covert blessings to others through prayer, meditation, and thought. My power lies in my ability to release my need to be recognized.

October 1

Today I choose to be SEEKING SOLITUDE. I retreat from the perpetual flows of activity in the external world to the seclusion of my own space and energy. From a quieted mind, I receive Divine Intuition and enlightened understanding. By dampening the influx of sensory distractions, I fine-tune the channels thru which I tap Higher Wisdom. My power lies in my ability to embrace the opportunity of aloneness.

October 2

Today I choose to be CALM IN THE MIDST OF CHAOS. I AM unaffected by the moods and energies of those around me. I maintain my frequency despite the presence of many, mangled vibrations being broadcast in my range of reception. I refuse to imbibe any states of mind that originate from the outskirts of omniscience, instead allowing others' wavelengths to flow past me and not through me. My power lies in my ability to establish energetic boundaries.

October 3

Today I choose to be EMPATHIC. I easily sense others' feelings and frame of mind. I intuitively interpret the visible and invisible messages that are being communicated to me. I AM absorptive, a receiver for emotive energies, able to empirically identify with another's perceived reality. My power lies in my ability to pay attention to my extrasensory impressions.

October 4

Today I choose to be INCREASING. All that is good in my life expands. My blessings multiply. Health, love, and abundance flow to me in ever greater capacities. My prosperity proliferates. My power lies in my ability to attract like with like by giving more of that which I wish to receive.

October 5

Today I choose to be FREE. I may do as I wish and seek out the path that most pleases me. I Am self-governing, uninhibited by the insecurities, ignorance, or plights of others. I subscribe to my own beliefs, aligning with that which feels right to me. My power lies in my ability to allow others to be responsible for their own needs and feelings.

October 6

Today I choose to be A CELEBRATION. I'm not just living, I AM ALIVE! That within itself is enough for me to engage in some form of enjoyable activity. Today will become comparable to birthdays, holidays, and anniversaries all wrapped into one. Therefore, for no particular reason at all, I AM going to ceaselessly spoil myself, only displaying actions that mark my pleasure each and every moment. Without exception, every commemorated bash will be a carousel of epic, memorable, and breathtaking events intertwining excessive elation, exaggerated euphoria, and superfluous shopping sprees! My power lies in my ability to do at least one thing I love each day.

October 7

Today I choose to be INTENTION. I determine the direction of all thoughts and actions. I AM the center focus, the aim of cooperative psychological and spiritual efforts. I draw upon energy and attention in order to come into manifestation. My power lies in my ability to continue being the force that unifies the SELF.

October 8

Today I choose to be DESTINY. I AM well-designed and full of promise. I AM a positive outcome that already exists in the spiritual realm. I inevitably manifest my ultimate expression, unfolding perpetually, moment by moment. My power lies in my ability to realize that everything that has occurred to this point and everything that occurs in the future is an instrumental part to my actualization.

October 9

Today I choose to be LIGHT. I AM a radiant energy that illuminates everything around me. I create the best possible manifestation of my surroundings and reveal hidden beauty and knowledge simply by focusing myself on an object or being. I fearlessly slay any and all darkness, creating a presence of warmth, clarity, and vitality. My power lies in my ability to know that my vibrant physical expression is a product of my intrinsic brilliance.

October 10

Today I choose to LET IT BE. There is nothing on the face of this Earth that is worth me losing my cool. I AM my star player and I can't possibly expect others to truly understand where I'm coming from...especially considering I AM the ONLY person that possesses my perspective. I will no longer DEFEND my point of view, JUDGE my past, nor will I ATTACH any negative emphasis to the way I personally identify the externally physical and internally mental pressure I experience on a day-to-day basis. Doing so will simply offset my growth. My power lies in my ability to accept that with every breath I AM granted, I also become more alive.

October 11

Today I choose to be PROGRESSION. My developed movement will continue toward my predestined journey's end. My eyes are now open and my heart is pure. My life mirrors enlightened successions, one series at a time. I don't need to be attached to the obscurely remote future because I can only be where I AM. My power lies in my ability to know that the best preparation for tomorrow is doing my best today.

October 12

Today I choose to QUIET THE MIND. It has taken quite some time, pain, and shame but I've concluded that events prior to, as well as after this present moment, DO NOT EXIST anywhere else outside of my mind. I now know that thinking is an instrument that can only reside in my past or my future. I was once told to work the tool and not to allow the tool to work me. My energy is directed toward the expansion of my awareness, eliminating the associated drifting process my subconscious mind has a tendency of doing. My power lies in my ability to enjoy the PEACE of mind that comes through shifting from past-future cognitive mode into the eternal present of mental stillness.

October 13

Today I choose to be LIFTING WITH LOVE. I improve any given situation by channeling the highest frequency possible towards all those involved. I choose to cast positive regard onto my most challenging circumstances and in so doing I foster positive change. As I heighten my own frequency, all that I AM and all that I encounter will follow suit. My power lies in my ability to create internally that which I desire to achieve externally.

October 14

Today I choose to be HAVING A BIRD'S EYE VIEW. I distance myself from my ego's interpretation of events and make observations from a more elevated and evolved place. With my enhanced perception, I AM able to better see TRUTH and find meaning. My field of vision is so much more expansive when I increase my spiritual altitude. My power lies in my ability to view experiences from the perspective of my Higher Self.

October 15

Today I choose to be OSMOTIC. I absorb and transmit knowledge simply by being present. I seek not to cling to wisdom but to allow it to flow seamlessly through me. I serve as a medium for the enlightenment of others. My power lies in my ability to recognize that I AM constantly transacting energy with my surroundings.

October 16

Today I choose to be PROSPEROUS BY NATURE. I AM intrinsically prone to abundance. Wealth is in my blood; it is my birthright and my heritage. Affluence is my natural state of being. My power lies in my ability to identify as my Divine Self.

October 17

Today I choose to be IN LOVE AT FIRST SIGHT. I AM suddenly struck with an intensely enjoyable infatuation that refuses to be ignored. I have a deep, undeniable compulsion to create an opportunity or make a grand gesture, and I will follow it. My innermost drive draws me toward a new and exciting path, and it just feels right. My power lies in my ability to allow my spirit to run omnisciently rampant.

October 18

Today I choose to be SELFLESS. I realize that giving is not only more fun than receiving, it is an integral part of receiving. There are limitless ways in which I can support and assist others today, I need only look for opportunities and I will find them. Through praise, encouragement, and kindness, I will lift the spirits of those I encounter and demonstrate the best aspects of human nature. My power lies in my ability to be of service.

October 19

Today I choose to be VISUALIZATION. I mentally construct a physical image of my heart's desires, dwelling lavishly on the details. I can picture the textures, shapes, sounds, words, aromas, vibrations, movements and feelings that constitute my creation. My vision is so vivid, it seems as though that which I desire already exists. My power lies in my ability to exercise my mind's eye.

October 20

Today I choose to be INTUITIVE. I access my Higher Mind simply by asking for its assistance. Solutions and inspirations flow effortlessly to me. My Source guides me with gentle impulses and inclinations. My power lies in my ability to listen to my internal voice.

October 21

Today I choose to be MOTIVATED. There is a precious purpose to my goals. I have a deep-seated reason for choosing the path I have chosen, and I keep this objective at the forefront of my mind. I AM driven not by the results of achievement but rather by the implications of the results. My power lies in my ability to understand why I desire what I desire.

October 22

Today I choose to be A CHILD. I AM a joyous being, free of shame, free of prejudice, free of inhibitions. The world is a safe place where I can explore and grow. I find delight in the most nominal of adventures. I trust my instincts and love fearlessly. My power lies in my ability to adopt a playful approach to life.

October 23

Today I choose to be GENTLE. I take care in handling others, being cognizant of the fact that whatever wounds they have endured are likely well-hidden and easily overlooked. I AM sensitive to subjective truths, respecting the reality assigned to them by their possessors. I AM loving, even when confronting or disagreeing with someone. My power lies in my ability to masterfully employ tact in every encounter.

October 24

Today I choose to be LOVE. I broadcast positive energy to the world at large. I offer the best of myself to each situation, regarding others as highly as I regard myself. I handle all those I encounter with care and camaraderie. My power lies in my ability to perceive the Oneness of humankind.

October 25

Today I choose to TAKE THINGS IMPERSONALLY. I realize there is no benefit in emotionally attaching to others' choices. I understand that we all are subject to our own beliefs and act on our perceived truths. I allow those in my life to create their own paths and seek out the lessons they need to learn. My power lies in my ability to realize that my peace arises from internal rather than external sources.

October 26

Today I choose to be REVERENT. I respect others as I respect myself. I realize that I AM only as free as I allow others to be. I pursue my goals without infringing on anyone's liberties or beliefs. I embrace the fact that each individual is as unique and entitled as I AM. My power lies in my ability to regard every Being as a sovereign and significant entity.

October 27

Today I choose to be UNIVERSAL. Through the vastness of Spirit, I cross all cultures, creeds, and cosmos. I AM One with all, unique in manifestation but common in material makeup. I AM at once eternal and ephemeral, evidential and ethereal. My power lies in my ability to perceive my True Nature.

October 28

Today I choose to be CREATING A NEW HABIT. I dispel of undesired behaviors by replacing them with constructive activities and practices. My progressive choices proliferate and accrue, yielding positive change in my life. Each day, I become a better version of myself. My power lies in my ability to realize the opportunity present in every hour and every alternative.

October 29

Today I choose to be A HOT AIR BALLOON. I rise above the lower energies of the material world, gliding into the vast, open, ethereal realm. As I increase my altitude, I become more liberated and carefree. I AM buoyant, airy, and wondrous. My power lies in my ability to elevate myself by altering states of energy.

October 30

Today I choose to be A MAGNET. I naturally draw people, opportunities, and material things that are reflective of my state of being. I AM inherently attractive and perpetually attracting. The Divine Intelligence within me brings that which I AM attuned to within my reach. My power lies in my ability to exercise the laws that govern my higher workings.

October 31

Today I choose to be A METAPHYSICIAN. I generate healing through the forces of energy and electromagnetism. I treat disease and illness by attuning my vibrations to the frequency of health. I gain insight into my feelings by tuning into their physiological expressions. I address my unmet mental and spiritual needs that are manifesting as physical symptoms and sensations. My mind is my medicine; I am fully integrated. My power lies in my ability to have confidence in the Divine Intelligence of my body.

November 1

Today I choose to be PASSIONATE. I AM the vibration from which purpose is derived. I AM a coursing motivational force that beckons one to act. I AM the vehicle to a life of fulfillment and meaning. I AM metaphysical fuel. My power lies in my ability to serve as a catalyst.

November 2

Today I choose to be DETACHED. I do not take others' choices personally and I allow those in my life the space and autonomy to be as they choose. I perceive the world through a conscious lens, tempering my sentiments and opinions with understanding and acceptance. I do not cling to my desires, but rather allow them to manifest by creating clear channels through which creative energy can flow. My power lies in my ability to be of open heart and mind.

November 3

Today I choose to be AMBIANCE. I AM able to create any mood that I desire. I evoke spiritual states through my artistic physicality. I affect the energy of those around me by projecting my vibrations. My power lies in my ability to influence my environment.

November 4

Today I choose to PAY ATTENTION TO DETAIL. I realize that small things make big differences. I take the time to consider the finer points, perceiving that being conscientious now will prevent problems later. I relish in every aspect of my creations. My power lies in my ability to appreciate each piece that compromises the whole.

November 5

Today I choose to be SUPERNATURAL. There is no limit to what I AM able to manifest. My capacity to create transcends my intellectual abilities and the laws of nature. I AM the source of every material desire and experiential actuality. My power lies in my ability to connect with my higher self.

November 6

Today I choose to be A JOYRIDE. My travels are pure delight, even if my destination is unknown. I generate inspiration by seeking only to experience what there is to experience. The world is open to me and I go where my intuition leads me. My power lies in my ability to be carefree.

November 7

Today I choose to be APPRECIATIVE. I take time to recognize the value of things that have been granted to me. I AM thankful for the slightest of blessings. I AM surrounded by miracles. My power lies in my ability to see wonder in everything.

November 8

Today I choose to be HUMBLE. I AM the master of my ego. I have no need to prove to others who or what I AM. I seek only internal validation. My power lies in my ability to be quietly confident.

November 9

Today I choose to be DREAMING. My mind wonders the mystical depths of the collective unconscious, inspiring me with the most beautiful expressions of possibility. There is no limit to what I can imagine; the Universe is my palette. My power lies in my ability to visualize realities beyond my conscious experience.

CONCIOUS AWARENESS

REFLECTION:
1) Define conscious awareness.
2) When you're in the heat of the moment and awareness doesn't appear to be available, how do you respond?
3) Where are you purposely not being aware? What are you running and/or hiding from?
4) In what ways do you work to improve your sense of selfhood? (Yoga, meditation, reading, writing, etc.)
5) What are the benefits of being consciously aware versus the consequences of lacking presence of the things around and within us?
6) Who in your life possess the power of discernment, discretion, or judgment?

CHOOSE TO ACT:
1) Practice exploring what's possible. Don't be attached to what appears predicable. Be flexible in your thinking.
2) Practice discernment. Proclaim not just what you desire to do but also why, while determining what's best for self and others.
3) Practice self-awareness and self-reflection. It's less about being self-righteous and more about doing what's best.

<u>WISDOM</u>

November 10

Today I choose to be WISE. I shrewdly make use of the lessons I have attained to this point. I recognize situations for what they are and instinctively know how to proceed based on prior experience and present discernment. I have expansive insight into problems, their causes, and their solutions, as I AM the possessor of lifetimes of knowledge, and I've seen it all before. My power lies in my ability to apply that which I have learned.

November 11

Today I choose to WALK BY FAITH...NOT BY SIGHT. What I hear and see are not always what I perceive them to be. I have no desire to take anything to heart because nothing outside of me is personal. My body was and is uniquely designed for the specifications of my deliberately intended purpose for being. I accept this challenge and refuse to hold myself accountable for standards imposed upon me by anything or anyone outside of myself. I will conjure up the courage to put my complete trust and confidence in the catalyst responsible for my existence. My power lies in my ability to know that my mind is an everlasting habitat that will endure the test of time, unlike the rotting and decaying organic matter found in this physical world that will endure the test of time.

November 12

Today I choose to SEE THE BIGGER PICTURE. I realize that everything makes more sense when considered from macroscopic perspective. I acknowledge that my destiny is comprised of both my adversities and my triumphs. Where I AM now is not a conclusive experience but rather a single aspect of a more elaborate plot that will unfold in time. My power lies in my ability to embrace the learning opportunity that is this moment and patiently await more knowledge and blessings.

November 13

Today I choose to be THE BOTTOMLINE. Throughout my life, I've endured my fair share of failure. I've seen any and every example of how life shouldn't be lived. Although I say that with all due respect, the fact of the matter is, I can't learn how to live my life by solely examining visually the way someone else is living theirs. My vision can only be seen through my eyes and my purpose can only be fulfilled through my animated intention for being. I take pride in following my first mind; it's my personal connection to the divinely intelligent, infinitely powerful source of contentment. My power lies in my ability to know that in the end, all things will be okay.

November 14

Today I choose to be OBJECTS IN MIRROR ARE CLOSER THAN THEY APPEAR. My approach to the road of life has become fearlessly cautious. I've engraved an amplified alertness into my conscious and subconscious mind because I realized that while the convexity of my eyes gives me a useful field of view, they also make objects appear smaller. Since smaller-appearing objects seem farther away than they actually are, I've unknowingly made maneuvers and lane changes assuming the adjacent life form(s) was a safe distance behind; when in fact, they were a tad bit closer. In turn, I caused chaos and commotion in the lives of others as well as my own. So to avoid future crashing and burning, I allow warning to serve as a reminder while operating and navigating this vehicle of mine. My power lies in my ability to know that at times, less is more but ignorance is never bliss.

November 15

Today I choose to be NO ROOM FOR ERROR. Life is an extreme sport and delusion is always busier than truth. The existence for being, naturally actualizes perpetual transitional phases, which typically yield uncertainty, confusion, misjudgment, and wild and fierce fanaticism. I will use the interval between the decay of the old and the formation and establishment of the new to inspire an anticipatory approach to all things and people. Instead of just sitting around talking or thinking about what I desire to be, I actively do things that further my cause. My power lies in my ability to know that I'll never get a second chance to make a first impression.

November 16

Today I choose to be RISK VERSUS REWARD. I had to realize that I couldn't just do whatever I wanted simply because I felt like it. It appears as if all choices in life are miraculously attached to some outcome...albeit a consequence or a dividend. Through experience, I've concluded that I AM not best suited for the aftermath of unconscious actions, you know, the decisions that stem from unreasonable expectations. I would rather take my chances using my power to select intentional planning above all other forms logical/illogical reasoning. My power lies in my ability to know that understanding behavior equates to avoiding danger.

November 17

Today I choose to be EMOTIONAL INTELLIGENCE. In my past, my cognition, thinking, speaking, and acting was without the inclusion of rationality. My alleged beliefs and opinions were typically given through the inadequate use of reason, dramatic impulsive distress, and/or cognitive deficiency. Over time, I couldn't help but conclude that those behaviors were not of much use to me pertaining to the manifestation of my goals. By process of elimination, I've developed the ability, capacity, and skill to evaluate my feelings and react objectively. I have a more effective understanding of who and what I AM. My power lies in my ability to manage risks and avoid hassles by viewing the big picture and not just some isolated incident that stems from a deeper-rooted cause.

November 18

Today I choose to be A PROCRASTINATOR. I've been known to defer actions and seemingly delay forward progress due to the fact that I AM never hurried by constraining myself to the laws of time, and the perceptions of others pertaining to me at best means little to nothing. People tend to accuse me of putting things off too much and not caring enough. They have gotten so caught up into this microwave society always wanting for something, doing a whole lot of nothing, which typically leaves them empty and unfulfilled. I just can't convince myself to identify anything as a lost opportunity; so I'll continue to operate at my own pace. There isn't a pressure immense enough to ever burst my pipes. I'll remain steadfast in my approach, confident in the inner essence that fuels me, and will attack all situations, scenarios, and people with a patient urgency. My power lies in my ability to know that regardless of how hot the heat is, I will never leave the kitchen.

November 19

Today I choose to be PRUDENCE. I remember a time in my past when I would find myself saying, "I should have seen that coming!" after negative events occurred in my life. Then I would proceed to bash and blame myself for being less than what I knew I was. My days and nights were filled with heartache and problems simply because I failed to see the situation for what it really is. I was too busy playing the part of the person being preyed upon when viewing those places of previous activity that initially appeared hopeless. In retrospect, I'm confident that they were merely blessings in disguise. I've since grasped the cause-and-effect relationships that govern all reality. My power lies in my ability to raise my awareness of the long-term effects of my actions seeing beyond the moment and understanding the spiritual challenges in every instance before they can become the foundations of chaos and crisis.

November 20

Today I choose to be CONSCIOUS CONFINEMENT. The best of anything I've ever done was created in solitude. Gathering in fellowship is awesome and people are cool but there's nothing better than intentional isolation. I've acquired enough information from my experiences to know that apprehending myself to aloneness will give me time for thought, the capacity to create, and doing so will allow me the aptitude to unwind and find/create peace. Quieting my space also helps me to appreciate the smaller things that tend to get lost in the uproar of life's everyday struggles. My power lies in my ability to manufacture moments geared toward the reflection of what I've done, why I did it, and how I will learn from it.

November 21

Today I choose to be LOSING SOME TO WIN SOME. Allegedly, it's not possible to win all the time. In this life, every path I take will be sure to have its fair share of puddles. I must remain cognizant that there is always light at the end of every tunnel. Regardless of how bad I want what I don't currently have, there is absolutely nothing wrong with where I AM, who I AM, or what I AM! I will remain immeasurably optimistic knowing that where there's a will, a way will be sure to follow and all circumstances, inadvertent of my personal opinion, will create blessings in disguise. My power lies in my ability to detach my emotions from all things that are transitory and subject to decay, spoil, or destruct.

November 22

Today I choose to be FREE TIME. This temporal length of events is typically spent away from business, work, and/or domestic chores. If eating, sleeping, and education aren't classified in the "LEISURE" category, when are these moments of life ever really without charge? Those activities pretty much consume each moment of my awakened life. Everything is seemingly attached to some form of consequence or reward. Therefore, I will choose to use the duration of my days focused on feelings that are complimentary and derived from love. My power lies in my ability to know that even when I AM not being compensated with monetary gains, my existence of space will always remain priceless!

November 23

Today I choose to be TRANSMUTING. I speak of what I desire, not of what I despise. I express appreciation for things in my world that give me joy rather than dwelling in complaint about the things that bring me pain. I proactively look for the good in people and easily eschew the bad. My power lies in my ability to turn negatives into positives.

November 24

Today I choose to be A DONATION. I selflessly give of my time, my love, and my possessions. I revel in the knowledge that something I have may be of great benefit to another. I detach from my contribution, asking only that the Universe see to it that my gift will go on to serve someone's best interest. My power lies in my ability to create space in my life for increasing abundance.

November 25

Today I choose to be MYSTICAL. I entertain the most fanciful capacities of my beliefs. I decipher the magic in the mundane, the divine in the day-to-day, and the calling in the commonplace. I practice the art of the connecting with the supernatural. My power lies in my ability to romance the spirit.

November 26

Today I choose to be ASTROLOGICAL. I easily make sense of the cycles of energy and stages of development that I encounter on my journey. I interpret the place and positioning of sacred expressions in my life to gain deeper insight into who I AM and where I'm going. I understand the influence of other realms on my present experiences. My power lies in my ability to be divine.

November 27

Today I choose to be ON AUTOPILOT. I trust that I will receive Divine Guidance at the exact moment that I need it. I refrain from analyzing and anticipating the unknown, thereby clearing the channel for spontaneous wisdom to flow. I let go of the necessity to control future circumstances, knowing that I will have everything I need as the need arises. My power lies in my ability to check my baggage and enjoy the flight.

November 28

Today I choose to be MEDIATING. I bring peace to others by helping them understand and respect differing points of view. I intervene on behalf of the Greater good, directing those I serve toward their higher selves. In bridging communication gaps, I facilitate agreement and reconciliation. My power lies in my ability to create opportunity out of opposition.

November 29

Today I choose to be ORGANIC. I evolve into my highest potential, untainted by caustic or artificial influences. I grow, thrive, and blossom by the sheer power of my innate programming. I yield the greatest harvest by cultivating my most natural Self. My power lies in my ability to use the resources already in my possession.

November 30

Today I choose to be REACHING OUT. I identify opportunities in which I can be of service and express my desire to help. I promote higher ways of living to others, inviting them onto the path of Divine Wisdom. I let it be known that I AM here, I AM available, and I care. My power lies in my ability to initiate connections.

December 1

Today I choose to be TEACHING. I proffer knowledge as a means of elevating the degree of collective consciousness and evolution. I demonstrate new means of perceiving, thinking, and creating. I foster another's learning process by sharing my own lessons and awakenings. My power lies in my ability to facilitate higher levels of understanding for those who seek my guidance.

December 2

Today I choose to be ACCREUING. As the years go by, I incrementally get stronger, wiser, and more whole. The small steps I have taken in days past collect and accumulate to yield an extraordinary evolvement in my Total Self. Time is my ally and the longer I mature, the better I get. My power lies in my ability to account for even the slightest of improvements when calculating my progress to this point.

December 3

Today I choose to be SMILING. I greet the world with a warm and welcoming countenance. I preemptively express the physical equivalent of that which I desire to experience emotionally. With my simple gesture, I create uplifting physiological changes in myself and lay the foundation for positive social interactions with others. My power lies in my ability to put my best face forward.

December 4

Today I choose to be A MESSENGER. I use my voice to channel Divine Love and guidance onto others. My words engender, encourage, and enlighten. Through conversation, I plant seeds of wisdom and insight in the minds of others. My power lies in my ability to sense what needs to be said.

December 5

Today I choose to be A LEADER. I initiate action and provide guidance to others. I have a vision and I understand what's needed to make it actualize. I AM able to achieve great things by creating an image of the future and directing my team's energy toward that image. My power lies in my ability to inspire and connect with others.

December 6

Today I choose to ALLOW MY DESIRES TO COME TO ME. I realize that in recklessly chasing or hunting my dreams, I act from a place of fear rather than faith. I opt instead to be certain of my aspired blessings, connecting with them through mental and spiritual means rather than through physical manipulation of circumstances. I AM Divinely Guided to take actions that result in seamless manifestation of my wishes. My power lies in my ability to release my grip on my external world, thereby opening the Divine Channels by which I receive.

December 7

Today I choose to be AN AMPLIFIER. I make greater that which is already being broadcast. I enhance the signal of frequencies so that they may be perceived and enjoyed by a wider audience. I AM able to transmit an unlimited range of vibrations in grand measure and magnitude. My power lies in my ability to plug-in to The Source.

December 8

Today I choose to be SEEING MYSELF IN OTHERS. I acknowledge that every person present in my life has a lesson to offer me. I have attracted these particular individuals because at some level, they reflect a part of my psyche, perhaps a part as yet unrecognized. I accept that even my most undesired relational dynamics are of my own creation. My power lies in my ability to determine which of my own beliefs are manifesting in each relationship.

December 9

Today I choose to be RECREATING. I AM perpetually in the process of drawing good into my life. Anything that I perceive as having lost I can again possess in finer and better form. The Universe is my provider. My power lies in my ability to believe that I have access to infinite abundance.

December 10

Today I choose to be A BLESSING. God's favor and protection has been on and around me my entire life. Every wish that I have ever prayed for has either already come true or is in the process of manifesting. I have no room to display any negative emotions/actions, complain, or to be jealous of anything or anyone. I will use my gifts to better serve myself as well as those around me. My power lies in my ability to know that the greatest gifts are not found in what we receive from others, but instead, they are located in what we GIVE to others.

December 11

Today I choose to be A PRESENCE OF MIND. When I encounter a crisis, I will work to maintain control of self. When I experience states of emergencies, I do not perceive the pressure to be stress. Instead, I will view these circumstances as probabilities for prosperity, which will guide me to do the right thing. I've learned that my biggest secret to success is a combination of incarcerating myself to every instant and making decisions each moment that will make me proud to be me later. My power lies in my ability to know that although 'I am' in the world, I AM not of this world!

December 12

Today I choose to be FORMING IDEAS INTO FULFILLMENT. My dreams and aspirations are rooted in the purity of the Universe. I will not allow the seemingly infinite variety of impediments get in my way...not doubts nor fears! I will forever be inspired by my brilliant thoughts, innovative ideas, and lofty goals. My power lies in my ability to bring spiritual and physical realms together, yielding courage and commitment to actualize my thoughts, accomplish my goals, and achieve my dreams.

December 13

Today I choose to be THE POWER OF WORD. Not only have I abused myself, I have completely misused my personally declared egotistical truths to curse, to blame, to find guilt, and to destroy others. I was conscious-stricken of spreading personal poison in efforts to express the anger, jealousy, and hate that I've allowed in my own life. Now that I AM cognizant of my wrongdoings, I will carefully select my choice of expressions ensuring that everything I say is backed with love. My power lies in my ability to look at my everyday human interactions eliminating the pure contamination of gossip from my thoughts and conversations.

December 14

Today I choose to be A FERTILE MIND. My brain is the equivalent to the plentiful soils of the Earth and my thoughts are seeds that are perpetually being planted. Even when I'm unaware, my current opinions, ideas, and concepts will lead to my future harvest; or lack thereof. My words I will choose wisely and my actions sensibly. Casting anything but affluent and prosperous wishes on others and myself, is simply unacceptable. My power lies in my ability to focus on breeding thoughts of lively energy and excitement enabling me to grow luxuriantly and profusely.

December 15

Today I choose to be SHARING THE FLAME. It is a known fact that a single candle lessens the darkness of space but no amount of darkness can extinguish a flickering flame. I will become that candle serving the family of humankind with my brilliance. I AM aware of the excessive blessings that have been bestowed upon my life and administering those gifts to others is not optional. I will continue to diminish my selfish nature by using the tools of clear thinking and clairvoyance, which will guide my calculated steps. My power lies in my ability to envision openings and opportunities in the world for the global distribution of spiritual awareness.

December 16

Today I choose to be PRACTICAL. I realize that my knowledge is only of benefit when applied. Studying is imperative, but it is only half of the process. I must use my insightful intelligence in order to unleash its potential. My power lies in my ability to transact my theories and ideas in everyday situations.

December 17

Today I choose to be CENSORING MYSELF. I recognize that, for better or worse, my words have implications. I know that criticizing, condemning, and complaining will not only fail to solve my problems but will also attract more negativity into my experience. Instead, I will use my voice to claim goodness and positive changes in my life. My power lies in my ability to think before I speak.

December 18

Today I choose to be INGENIOUS. Just because I did something in a certain way yesterday, doesn't mean I should do it the same way today. I AM full of new and innovative approaches and I easily find shortcuts and solutions. I AM resourceful, clever, and inventive. My power lies in my ability to be creative.

December 19

Today I choose to be FRESH AIR. I AM breezy and reviving. I gently do away with staleness and stagnancy. I refresh all who seek my solace. My power lies in my ability to create new energy.

December 20

Today I choose to be PASSING THE TEST. Once I decide to live by faith, my ideologies will inevitably be challenged. Any perceived obstacle I encounter is actually an opportunity for me to prove my belief in the Divine Order. Difficult times will serve only to strengthen my convictions rather than deteriorate them. My power lies in my ability to prepare for my exam.

December 21

Today I choose to be A WITNESS. I see first—hand the wondrous capacity of belief and I share my observations with others. I AM always on the lookout for miracles and magic. My testimony encourages those around me to take hold of their own supernatural abilities. My power lies in my ability to help others discover TRUTH.

December 22

Today I choose to be LIVING SIMPLY. I take pleasure in small things and seek to be present in each moment. My desire is to live with elegance rather than extravagance. I realize that there are limits to the benefits of multitasking. My power lies in my ability to pursue quality over quantity.

December 23

Today I choose to be A CHESS PLAYER. I can visualize the steps I must take in order to obtain my objective. My strategy is clear to me and my every move is precise. Victory is in my sights. My power lies in my ability to perceive.

December 24

Today I choose to be GIVING BACK. I AM abundantly blessed and I generously share my wealth. I see the potential in others and look for ways to support and encourage them. I plant seeds along my journey, creating opportunities for those who follow to be sheltered and provided for. My power lies in my ability to show thanks and respect for my good fortune through altruism.

December 25

Today I choose to be ELATED. My world is free of struggle and stress and I reject all feelings of angst. I anticipate the best possible outcome for all of today's endeavors. My spirit is light and my heart is open. My power lies in my ability to expect to encounter only good things and I seek the goodness in every experience.

December 26

Today I choose to be ATTENTION. I AM able to direct myself toward any number of stimuli, however, I AM selectively focused on only positive things. The more of myself I give to a particular concept, the more of that concept I attract. When I apply myself to the things I desire, I catalyze their manifestation into my experience. My power lies in my ability to entertain only that which serves me by filtering out all negative ideas and perceptions.

December 27

Today I choose to be OXYGEN. I AM a necessary element of the world around me and I benefit everyone I encounter by offering energy, breath, and vitality. I AM life-affirming, omnipresent, and connected to everything on Earth. I give of myself without asking for anything in return. I AM created and recreated and I AM cycled and recycled in a process designed to perpetuate every living being. My power lies in my ability to facilitate spiritual thrift in the physical realm.

December 28

Today I choose to be AN ARISTOCRAT. I AM privileged, noble, and prosperous. I live a life full of favor and abundance. I AM a most high being. My power lies in my ability to recognize my worth.

December 29

Today I choose to be A BANK. I have more riches than imaginable and I never stop growing. I benefit by benefitting others. I AM a source of prosperity for myself and those around me. My power lies in my ability to provide opportunity and service.

December 30

Today I choose to be AN INCUBATOR. I create a nurturing mental environment that keeps and prospers my dreams and desires. With my thoughts I cast a warm, nourishing light upon my budding aspirations. My mind is a place perfectly calibrated to allow my ambitions and ideas to take root and thrive. My power lies in my ability to hold a positive vision.

December 31

Today I choose to be ON THE BRINK. All of my efforts to this point have brought me to the threshold of my dreams. My future is starting now. All signs are pointing toward blessings to ensue. My power lies in my ability to recognize the subtle ways in which my desires are already manifesting.

WISDOM

REFLECTION:
1) Define wisdom.
2) What is the greatest gift wisdom has yielded you?
3) How likely are you to follow your intuition? Why or why not?
4) How has wisdom helped you create opportunities out of opposition?
5) How do you generate peace and harmony for self/others?
6) Does your capabilities stem from desperation or deep understanding?

CHOOSE TO ACT:
1) Practice seeking understanding from perspectives aside from your own.
2) Practice being persistent. They say experience is our greatest teacher.
3) Practice using your body of knowledge and principles to make sound decisions that derive from purpose.

ABOUT THE AUTHOR

Marcus Lucy is a life coach, personal trainer, and motivational speaker in the Chicago metropolitan area. For the past 15 years, Marcus has dedicated his life to helping others realize and achieve greatness and complete wellness. Graduating from Concordia University with a degree in Exercise Science, he went on to excel as Director of Fitness for a national fitness brand, being acknowledged as an exemplary leader and personal trainer. His passion to be a positive force in others' lives prompted him to obtain his Life Coach Certification from Accomplishment Coaching, helping hundreds of individuals break past the self-inflicted barriers in their lives. Marcus continues to nurture growth in people of all age groups through various mentorship programs, speaking engagements, and coaching seminars.

Learn more about Marcus Lucy at www.marcuslucy.com.

Made in the USA
Lexington, KY
19 March 2017